American Justice?

Paul Brakke

with Gini Graham Scott, PhD

TouchPoint
Press

AMERICAN JUSTICE?
by Paul Brakke
Published by TouchPoint Press
4737 Wildwood Lane
Jonesboro, Arkansas 72401
www.touchpointpress.com

ISBN 13: 978-0692710685
ISBN 10: 069271068X

Ebook Edition
True Crime Series, Vol. 2

TouchPoint Press books may be purchased in bulk or at special discounts for sales promotions, gifts, fund-raising, or educational purposes. For details, contact the Sales and Distribution Staff: TouchPoint Press, 4737 Wildwood Lane, Jonesboro, Arkansas 72401 or info@touchpointpress.com. Requests accepted via fax: 662-510-0302.

Cover Design: Colbie Myles, colbiemyles.com

First Edition

Printed in the United States of America.

This book is dedicated to my wife Carol, whose previously untold and intolerable suffering catalyzed its creation. I only wish I could have shielded her from what befell her instead.

CONTENTS

This book could only have been rendered readable due to major and truly remarkable editing efforts by Rob Levey, the TouchPoint Press staff, and, most significantly, Elizabeth Zack (BookCrafters LLC).

PROLOGUE

My wife and I went through an unexpected, bizarre, and frightening ordeal. Never in our wildest imaginings did we expect anything like this to happen to law-abiding citizens like ourselves. And as the crisis proceeded and progressed in its intensity, my wife and I reached the unfortunate conclusion that our faith, and our naïve trust, in America's legal and justice system was misplaced. We had expected to be treated fairly and justly by our community, our society, and those who serve to protect us. That didn't happen.

The event changed us profoundly. The two of us will never be the same again. Nor will our lives or our lifestyle.

My goal for writing this book is to make sure what happened to my wife and me — an experience that went further awry because of a naiveté and unfamiliarity that is common in the general population with the workings of the legal and justice systems — is not the kind of experience that ever happens to you or beloved members of your family.

But before I reveal what we underwent, I feel it's best to provide you with a little personal history as to who I am, and where I come from. This way, you can understand and appreciate who I am. Who my wife is. You'll have the benefit of knowing that my wife and I never had any negative experience with the legal/justice system prior in our lives. Indeed, by the time our crisis happened, we were both in our later years, having lived rich, full and what most would term as "normal" lives.

I was born in New York City in 1949 to Eastern European parents. I lived there until I was fifteen. I then spent the next twelve years in or around Philadelphia, and I received my Ph.D. at the University of Pennsylvania in 1976.

After that, I spent time doing post-doctoral work in several places, including Nashville, where I met my wife, Carol, and where we married in 1983. It was a second marriage for each of us, and we were thrilled to have found our lifelong partner.

We moved to Galveston, Texas, where we would happily spend the next twenty-two years. I had accepted a position as a faculty member in the physiology department of a medical school there. I would be doing muscle research there, and for much of that time Carol would work for me as a research associate (technician).

On the island of Galveston, we led an idyllic existence. With our new home just two blocks away from the lab where we worked, we had no commute. This new location allowed us to go home for lunch every day. Spending so much time together in a laidback community on the shore was like a dream. We cherished our time there.

Sadly, that time came to end. Carol and I made the difficult decision we had to move upon receiving the news that our institution was building a Bio-Safety Level 4 facility less than a block from where we worked eight hours a day. Worse, its location was only three blocks away from where we lived!

Bio-Safety Level 4 (BSL-4) indicates that the facility is considered safe enough to work with the most dangerous microbes known to man, including anthrax, Ebola, smallpox, and bubonic plague. While Carol and I had no concerns about the safety of such microbes within the Safety Level 4 building, we had real concerns about the individuals who would be working with such organisms. At the time, we heard true stories of some researchers' cavalier attitudes that affected how those researchers handled these microbes. The news shocked us to our cores.

For example, one researcher was failing to declare the vials of such microbes when traveling on well-known commercial airline flights! (Fortunately, the authorities uncovered what was going on, and stopped this behavior.) And the news was just as bad when it came to those researchers who lived close to us: One neighbor was taking the microbes home and storing them in his home freezer (much to his own wife's dismay).

Carol and I were unable to fathom why such researchers felt that they knew better than the regulators as to what was safe. Due to how they were handling these specimens, they were potentially exposing others to fearsome, worrisome, and often fatal diseases.

Compounding our concern over this situation was the fact that our town of Galveston was located on the tip of a barrier island. The island only had two bridges and a ferry leading to the mainland. In the event of any microbe leak, authorities on the Texas mainland would quarantine the island — thereby forcing its inhabitants to endure continual exposure to potentially lethal microbes in order to protect those on the more populated mainland. While we understood that this would be done to help prevent the spread of disease, Carol and I were not comfortable about being put at risk like this because of where we lived.

Another new factor influencing us to move was the arrival of a new department chairman. He was one of the most disagreeable individuals I have ever known, and his presence was greatly reduced the pleasure I derived from my day-to-day work.

So when the opportunity arrived, I jumped at the invitation to join the University of East Kansas for Medical Sciences (UEKMS) in Big Pebble. This was in the late summer of 2005. This institution had just recruited two senior cardiovascular researchers with whom I had been collaborating, and accepting the position offered me a rare opportunity to change institutions as a senior faculty member.

Carol and I promised each other that we would attempt to continue the kind of lifestyle we so cherished on Galveston Island by living close to my new workplace. Still, it was not without some trepidation that we agreed on the move.

Moving would be an extremely difficult transition for Carol. She and I had landscaped our home in Galveston together, and taking my avid-gardener-of-a-wife away from her homegrown and conceived garden was similar to yanking a favorite well-rooted plant out of the ground.

However, we went to tour our potential new community, and found a neighborhood in Big Pebble very close to my new workplace that seemed suited to us. There was a very nice house for sale that was just a ten-minute walk away from the building I would be working in. To this day, I believe Carol and I would not have moved had we not found and purchased that house.

Late in the summer of 2005, we moved to 341 Pearly Lane in Big Pebble. While we hired movers to take care of getting most our things there, we had a vast number of exotic and grown plants that we had put in ourselves and nourished for years. We did not want to leave these treasured and sentimental specimens behind. So we dug up and moved a lot of our plants to Big Pebble ourselves, via a U-Haul truck. It took three separate overnight drives from Galveston to get those plants to Big Pebble, but it was worth it.

So it would be Carol and me, two cats, and dozens of our plants that would call our place in Big Pebble "home."

Our new community welcomed us — even before we were settled in. Neighbor Johnny Boyle approached after my first plant haul, and offered to keep the plants watered when he discovered I would be making more trips back to Galveston to get the rest. And after another one of those plant hauls, neighbor Tina White, came over to greet me.

Tina lived right across the street from us, where our two houses abutted at an intersection. She seemed friendly enough at the time, although she and

I did not have much in common. Tina was a mom in her late thirties raising three kids, two boys and a girl, with her husband William. She was attractive, and always dressed in the latest fashions. She and Carol started to speak often, and after telling Carol she was a photographer, she showed her some of her work. Carol told me it was quite artistic.

Tina's husband William was an environmental lawyer in his forties. He regularly supervised the kids in the afternoon when he came home, most often keeping his attention on the two youngest children, Wayne and Missy.

Tina told us her son Wayne, a first grader in 2008, was a "special needs child." My wife found him to be shy, kind, and very considerate. He always called Carol "Mrs. Carol," and my wife adored him.

Carol didn't feel the same affection for Missy, the youngest of the three children. She was at the age where she had daily temper tantrums, and her shrieks often echoed across the street.

As for the White's oldest boy Willie, he was an avid basketball player. He played every day, first in his own yard and then in the intersection (more on that later). Right from the start, Willie never looked Carol quite in the eye, and always tried to avoid her.

Moving Pangs

Leaving her home of over twenty years made Carol sad. She was quite attached to the home and its garden, and our lifestyle and community there. So she and I took pains to spend a lot of our first year at Pearly Lane fixing up the house and yard to her liking. Carol had a sprinkler system installed so she could fashion and maintain a garden, which she did. She put in some winter jasmine in front of the house, placing them so the plants would droop prettily over a brick wall toward the sidewalk. In the winter, the jasmine sported spectacular yellow blooms.

She put in many other plantings in the back yard, and that yard blossomed into a real joy for the two of us. Together we planted a potted Japanese maple we were fond of in the back, where it thrived beyond our wildest expectations. I also installed brick paths around the periphery of the back yard, and became as proud of the job I did there as I was of brick and stonework I had installed in the yard of our Galveston home.

One of the best parts about our new home was that the room we spent the most time in opened up to the yard through some French doors, giving us a beautiful view. Better yet, the master bedroom, located in a rear corner of the house, had three full windows on the back wall that allowed us to lie in bed and have a gorgeous view of our backyard.

By the time we were done with all this work, Carol started to like the house much more, and miss her Galveston home much less.

For about half a year in our new location, Carol worked a desk job. When she decided that shuffling papers wasn't for her, she retired. She now had a lot of time on her hands at home with little companionship, so we picked out a little dog from the pound in May and brought her home. Sandy became Carol's perfect companion.

All in all, I have to say our first two years on Pearly Lane were nice ones. We had little to complain about. Unfortunately, that would change.

PART I

CHAPTER 1: THERE GOES THE NEIGHBORHOOD!

In 2007, our neighborhood experience began to change. College kids living right next door to us moved away, and renters Brody and Gina Odom moved in with their two children, Odie and San.

Bearded and sporting shoulder-length red hair that he tucked into a ponytail, Brody Odom was the self-styled leader of a part-time rock band that included his wife. While the band did not practice next door, we found Brody loud enough on his own, talking loudly on his cell phone in the front yard most of the time. He was around so much that Carol and I doubted he had a full-time job. His wife Gina worked full-time as a paralegal, taking off so early in the family car each day that we rarely ever saw her in the daytime.

The Odom's children, Odie and San, soon became good friends with the rest of the kids in the neighborhood. They frequently played with the Whites' children, as well as the Knights' children who lived next door to them.

Assistant City Manager Billy Knight lived in the house on the other side of the Odoms. Billy and his wife Bettie had a son and daughter roughly the same age as the Odoms'. Their kids behaved well when they knew they were being observed — but much of the time, that didn't apply. Often outside unsupervised and left to their own devices, they followed the lead of the rest of the group that was hanging out — and that wasn't always an optimal situation.

The first thing that caught out attention was that a large group of kids often started actively playing in the street intersection in front of our homes. That worried Carol and me. The intersection was T-shaped, with our house located at the top of the T. There was only one stop sign in this widened intersection, and that was for drivers coming up the T. Drivers at the top of the T were not required to stop, even if they were turning to go down the T. Maybe the increased play in the intersection wouldn't have been so concerning if the area was marked for safety, but there were no "Children at Play" signs. Nor were there pedestrian crosswalks. To top it off, often the parents of those playing outside in the middle of the street weren't there to supervise. Without parents present to supervise and draw their kids' attention to approaching cars, the youngest of the kids weren't always paying as much attention to vehicular traffic as they should have because of their age.

Now, children had been playing in the intersection ever since Carol and I had moved in. But in the beginning, it was just a few older kids from the neighborhood playing there from time to time. It seemed that with the influx of new kids into the neighborhood, every time Carol and I looked out the window or ventured outside, the kids were choosing repeatedly, to get together and chase each other in the middle of the street intersection in the front of our home.

We couldn't understand it: There was a local school playground empty after-hours that was located right down the street, but they were choosing to play in this intersection, where all sorts of things could happen.

With Carol home full-time now, and the children being excessively noisy because of their large number and the excitement they derived from their outside activities, it wasn't long before Carol started to come out to ask the kids to keep the noise level down and to warn them of the danger their chosen place of play posed. But the children didn't care; Carol wasn't their parent, and they weren't going to listen to her.

It didn't help that their parents didn't back Carol at all. In fact, the exact opposite happened: The grown adults in the neighborhood ignored her concerns entirely. Some even started to ridicule and try to intimidate her!

This happened first with Brody Odom. When he found out from Odie and San that Carol was expressing both her concern and unhappiness to his children, Brody reacted by intimidating my wife. At the time, I was unaware of what Brody was doing. Carol didn't tell me what was happening because she didn't want me to start disliking our neighborhood. I thought Carol's growing dislike of Brody was simply due to her dislike of his hippy-like appearance.

About a month after the Odoms moved in, Carol complained to Billy Knight about the amount of play going on in the intersection. After all, Knight was an assistant city manager, so he would be well aware of the city code. But Knight chose to ignore it as far as his children were concerned: He told Carol he wouldn't do anything to reduce the play in the intersection.

Carol and I couldn't believe it. A group of parents in their 30s or 40s was allowing their kids to play unsupervised in a street intersection.

Moreover, the parents didn't like, support, or approve of anyone who disagreed with their children's established routine!

Weren't the parents concerned about their children's safety? Cars frequently would dart through the intersection; *weren't the parents concerned that one of their kids might chase after an errant basketball or after each other in a game of tag and get hit by a car or truck?*

In other homes and neighborhoods, it is quite common for parents to let their children play in a fenced-in yard, their homes' driveways, or even in the middle of a quiet cul-de-sac while they are inside making dinner or tending to household matters. Playing in yards and driveways might involve a fall or a scraped-up ankle or hand; they don't pose the danger of being run down by a stranger neighbor unaware that a child is darting about in delight in the street!

When Carol asked William White why the kids chose the intersection to play instead of at the nearby playground, he responded with a firm, "The children have played there for twelve years, and they will continue to play there."

No bones about it: These neighborhood parents weren't going to budge when it came to the actions and chosen place for play by their children.

Childish Play Going Awry

At the end of September, Odie and another boy walked down the street, BB guns in hand. Brody Odom was in his front yard, but didn't do anything to stop them. As they walked by our house, they shot at it, leaving a bullet hole in one of the windows. This scared Carol, and she called the police. They came but did nothing. Carol didn't tell me about the incident, worried that if I knew, I might pour kerosene on an already incendiary situation. Besides, she knew I was happy and had settled in quite nicely here, so I think she wanted to avoid shattering my own good image of our new neighborhood.

In October, Carol spied some kids jumping off a tall cinderblock wall in front of the Odoms' house into the street. Then they began throwing stuff at other kids walking by. Carol went outside and told them to cut it out, but her words had no effect. She then asked one of the boys whom she didn't know where he lived, but he refused to tell her. When Brody Odom heard her questioning the boy, he strode over from his yard where he had been watching and screamed at Carol, telling her she belonged

"…in an insane asylum or institution!"

By the end of October, the Odoms had placed a basketball hoop in front of their house in the street. It was another violation of city code, which stated "it is unlawful to place any sports equipment and any other article in the public rights-of-way of the city" and that basketball goals were only permitted on a cul-de-sac or dead-end street. Carol didn't know quite what to do. Having the hoop there would only mean more running, dashing about, and active play in the road! But Brody had been intimidating her for months now, and she didn't feel that she could have a rational, adult conversation with him. So she chose an indirect path to avoid confrontation: she put out a sign that the basketball hoop in front of the Odoms' house violated city code. It wasn't the best choice on Carol's part, but she wanted to get her message across in a way that didn't involve direct person-to-person conversation — and unnerving conflict. The sign was ignored. And the Odoms couldn't have missed it.

After the Odoms refused to get the message, Carol called the police. They did next to nothing about the situation. The only consequence was that the Odoms moved the hoop so that it was halfway in their driveway, halfway in the street.

Better, but still falling short. Feeling bad about the growing tension between our family and the Odoms, Carol offered Gina Odom a couple of our plants as a friendly gesture in early spring, which Gina welcomed and planted in her front yard.

But even though fall and winter in our neighborhood had been uneventful, in March, Carol saw a bunch of the kids that included Willie White trying to tear up a stone wall on the property of a black family on the other side of the intersection. Their efforts scarred the wall, and the family did not repair the wall until the following October. After noticing this incident, Carol told our neighbor Tina about it at a suitable opportunity. Tina White refused to accept that her son Willie had anything to do with going into, and defacing, their neighbor's property. This was surprising, given that the neighborhood kids were always running into, and through, property that wasn't their own.

Growing Tension in the Neighborhood

New problems surfaced across the street at the Whites' home in May. One morning Carol looked out the window across the street, only to see a suitcase in the yard with lots of shirts strewn about. Tina had very obviously thrown her husband William out.

How would the children of the Whites react to this very evident hostility between their parents? Carol and I wondered, and worried. Children usually don't react well to parents splitting up, and this sometimes comes across in their attitudes and actions.

In June, the kids gathered over at the Odoms were using pogo sticks for several hours. It made a repetitive racket hour after hour. Carol tried to ignore the sound, but finally, she couldn't take it anymore. She got up from where she was reading in the front room and went over to complain. She told the children the noise was affecting her, and asked them if they would mind jumping on their sticks further off down the street. A few moments later, Billy and Bettie Knight came to knock at our door and complain to Carol that she had intimidated their child.

A few days later, Tina White's dog Trubbel, whom Tina had bought just a few months before, bit Carol. The bite drew blood. Trubbel was out loose because his owners never walked him; the Whites simply let him out loose to pee and poop wherever he liked. And that was on not only on his family's property, but also on the neighbors' property. This was especially annoying because the Whites never bothered to pick up the poop the dog left behind in neighbors' yards. It exasperated the neighbor living right next door to the Whites so much that she chose to install a fence to keep the Whites' dog (and other family's kids) out of her yard.

After she tended to the wound, Carol called to ask Tina if she could see proof of the dog's rabies vaccination so she didn't have to worry about catching the disease. Tina brought it over — along with her mother. And when Carol showed them the bite marks Trubbel had left on her, the mother-and-daughter team didn't believe Carol. They said the marks weren't from their dog.

Another day, Carol looked out the window of our home — only to see that the neighborhood children had placed a ramp on our driveway to vault with their bicycles right out into the street. *Our driveway* let me emphasize. Carol picked up the phone, and called the police to complain about a dangerous activity going on without permission in our yard. The police responded that the kids had rights as pedestrians — *rights that superseded motorist rights!*

Why wouldn't the local police support us against this intrusion, which was a type of trespassing and might pose a liability to us as homeowners? Carol and I worried that if the children injured themselves flying off the ramp, their parents might have their parents' insurance company sue us, as the injury would have happened on our property.

But all the police officers who spoke with Carol said was that the neighborhood association was a more appropriate place to raise such complaints. So I contacted the president of the Hidden Valley Neighborhood Association about the issues that we were constantly experiencing with the children's poor decision-making and street/property intrusions, and the lack of support we were getting back from their parents. The man told me that the association probably "…would not want to get involved." So it came as no surprise that although the man promised to stop by our house to speak further about the ongoing situation, he never did. All Carol and I received in response to our real concerns and lack of respect from the children and their parents was radio silence.

At this point in our tale, I'd like to emphasize that not all the children in our neighborhood were causing us problems; several of them were gems. The family who lived three doors down from the Whites homeschooled their seven kids. These children were well behaved and sweet. One of them, Mary, brought Carol cookies one time, and occasionally came over to visit with her. Carol really enjoyed these visits: She missed being a mom and raising a daughter, as her own daughter Donata was now full-grown and living far away.

However, this leads me into what happened in August. Carol grew concerned one day when she looked outside and saw Mary taking up with some of the kids whose behavior was usually both rowdy and unruly. She went outside, asked Mary to come with her, and then brought Mary to her parents' home. When the parents answered the door, she warned them that these other kids were likely to be bad influences on their own lovely and well-mannered child.

When Carol left their house to return home, Richard Butler, a, neighbor sitting in the screened-in porch of his home adjacent to the Whites' home yelled out, "Go home, Nazi!" at Carol, in full hearing of the kids still darting about in the street.

Carol was especially horrified at his accusation and name-calling — and she had good reason to be. Carol was born in 1937 in a small town in western Germany, and she still speaks English with a German accent. During part of World War II, Carol's family sent Carol and her brother off to Austria to be safer from the Allied bombings. These bombings had killed hundreds of thousands of German civilians, including some of Carol's relatives. To this day, Carol still remembers how frightened she was when, at the end of the war, her family had to surrender to Allied soldiers, as her family was afraid they would be killed or tortured.

At eighteen, Carol left for the United States to go to school. While in New York City, she met the man who became her first husband. He too was German. Carol then attended Columbia University and became educated about all the atrocities committed by the Nazis. Carol preferred the U.S. and its people to the Germans she had known. Carol stayed here, choosing to become became a citizen of the United States back in 1960.

Carol and her husband had two children together: a daughter and a son. Because the couple was appalled and affected by the actions of the Nazis, they chose to name their son "Henning," after Henning von Treskow, one of the co-conspirators in the failed attempt to assassinate Adolf Hitler.

So to be told, "Go home, Nazi" when she had chosen to leave her native country for over fifty years and become a citizen of the United States, proved particularly unconscionable to Carol. It was evident that this racist was victimizing her in this way because of both her accent and ancestry — neither of which Carol could do anything about.

Carol was older than neighborhood parents who were in their 30s raising kids, and she sounded like she "hailed" from Germany too. Undoubtedly, both age and ethnicity were working in this man's mind against Carol. Carol was a mother herself, a woman who had raised two lovely children. She knew what went into being a parent — and allowing children to play unsupervised in a street intersection, and also intrude into the neighbors' property and invade their privacy, was not characteristic of how most well-meaning parents raised their young. Carol was from a different generation. She had been raised with a lot of discipline and had raised her own children with more discipline than the children in Hidden Valley. She felt the parents here were being irresponsible.

Choosing not to confront Butler and escalate what had become an ugly situation, Carol gathered herself together and quietly proceeded on her way. But she didn't get far. Indeed, she didn't even reach our home before more antagonistic behavior reared its ugly head: Brody Odom strode up to Carol and, planting himself less than a foot in front of her, stared her down while saying nothing, absolutely nothing.

So ashamed and intimidated was my wife about this whole chain-of-events that Carol didn't tell me about these incidents with Butler and Odom for several months. It was only at that point that Carol also confided in me as well about the intimidating behavior directed at her by Brody Odom on several prior occasions.

"Get Her!"

It was now the case that every time Carol simply stepped out of our home when Willie White was outside, he would make aggressive arm motions, and then shielding motions, as if Carol was striking him. At the very sight of her, he would start screeching, "Here she comes!" and draw every other child's attention to her presence.

To be treated like this, and to be made to feel like an outcast or pariah in her own yard and neighborhood, angered Carol. She didn't let the boy know this, and did her best to ignore his behavior. She didn't even tell me about how she felt at the time.

When she found an opportunity, Carol approached the boy who seemed to be Willie White's closest friend and asked him why Willie was acting the way he was. All he told Carol was that, "Willie needed attention."

To me, this didn't seem like a good or smart way to get attention.

But since no adults told him to stop, Willie simply continued his hurtful behaviors. And his actions emboldened and inspired many of the other kids to treat my wife and our home poorly.

The neighborhood kids started ringing our doorbell and running away before Carol could open the door. When she was outside and there were no parents outside or looking, the kids made faces at her, and called her a "Nazi!" Again, this was always when no parents were looking or in hearing range.

At a few points, Carol complained afterwards to the children's parents — to no avail. The persecution just continued.

It got so bad that Carol finally asked me to have gates installed at the bottom of the steps leading up to our house in order to discourage kids from coming to ring our doorbell. *This* was the present she requested from me to celebrate our twenty-fifth wedding anniversary, and it was a real shot-to-the-heart indicator of how badly things were going in the neighborhood for Carol: *How could the children be intimidating my wife so badly that she would ask for gates as an anniversary present? They were just kids, right? What could be so scary or upsetting about them?*

Despite having some misgivings, I acquiesced. I wanted my wife to be happy, and the gates were what she said she wanted.

Hindsight...

Even though Carol had to ask me for gates, I never truly "got" how badly the kids were misbehaving, or how irresponsible their parents were about supervising them. In hindsight, I wish I had discussed the matter myself with some of the parents. As of this writing, and today as you are reading this narrative, I must tell you that I consider it a personal failing that I never did.

You might then be wondering how I did react when my own wife would tell me about the problems? Well, don't forget that in the beginning, Carol kept some of the most upsetting incidents to herself. Then, when she started to confide in me, I told her to "ignore" what was going on. I think I said, "Stop paying attention so much to the kids! Pay attention to your own issues instead." Sometimes, too, I tried to laugh it off, believing we should "…live and let live."

With the writing of this book, I apologize to my wife for not being intuitive enough to grasp the enormity of the situation at hand. I just didn't get it; I didn't understand. Not only was I preoccupied with my job and its demands, but I was also concentrating on forging a new life here in Big Pebble for us as our family's now-sole breadwinner. What Carol was telling me about seemed trivial in comparison to my own concerns, which I perceived to be more immediate and larger in scope and intensity.

Truth be told, I had no idea what lay in store for my wife — and by extension, me.

Yet even though I admit to being slow to grasp the enormity of what was going on, when the next phase of abuse happened, I stood by my wife's side and tried to hold her hand.

Unfortunately, that would prove to be physically impossible for part of the time.

CHAPTER 2: A NIGHTMARE ENSUES

October 23, 2008 began like any other day — except that I had a special treat for Carol on her birthday. I gave her a pretty green malachite necklace and earring set. She thanked me for the gift and put it on.

While I went to work at the lab, Carol spent much of her birthday at home reading and relaxing. It was only when she took out our dog Sandy for a walk in the afternoon that her peaceful day ended and everything began to fall apart.

As she walked around our neighborhood, she passed a group of kids. They began calling after her, "Nazi! Hey, Nazi. Nazi!"

Carol stayed quiet, but quickened her steps. She retreated to the safety of our house.

When I returned from work, Carol was walking pacing in the shaking and sweating. "The kids called me a Nazi when I walked past them with the dog," she finally managed. Her voice shook; she was very close to tears.

I stood there dumbfounded: *It was the first time Carol had told me about this racist abuse.* Up to now, the kids in the neighborhood had seemed mainly noisy and annoying to me as they threw basketballs at the hoop near our house. The expression of unprovoked hostility towards Carol appalled me. Completely.

I peered out of the window towards the street, and observed a half-dozen kids silently tossing basketballs for about five minutes.

How could it all seem so peaceful outside when it wasn't the case in my home?

Then, as I looked out the window of our home toward the children, a black sedan stopped in the intersection, picked up one of the younger kids, and made a U-turn. When the car passed by our home, the 7- or 8-year old boy in the backseat leaned far out of the right rear window and gave our house a Nazi salute.

I reared back visibly, in shock realizing the situation was every bit as bad as Carol had portrayed. Nonetheless, I tried to reassure Carol through my words, telling her, "It's just a young kid. It doesn't mean anything. Don't take it personally. Let's go out to eat together somewhere."

Carol couldn't put aside what happened. In a voice sounding a bit hysterical, she told me, "I've got to get away from all of this first. Be by myself for a bit. I can't take it anymore!"

I pleaded with her, using the voice of reason to say, "Don't go while you're so upset and those kids are still out there on the street."

But Carol insisted. And so shortly before six p.m. on her birthday — and without telling me where she would be going — she got into our car and backed out of the driveway. As she did, I made sure to stand at the front door and watch to make sure that the kids congregated in the street didn't hassle her as she pulled out.

The group of kids who were standing there left her alone.

Unfortunately, unknown and unseen by me because of where he was located, Willie White was sitting on a landscaping wall down the street. As my wife's car approached, he taunted her by throwing his arms in the air and making faces at her.

Carol told me what happened after.

She said she had had enough. She stopped the car, rolled down her window, and told the boy, "Stop it, or I'll complain to your parents."

Willie just continued to insult her, making faces and hollering at her before running away.

Unnerved and distraught from this encounter, Carol tried to turn around in a neighbor's driveway. Shaking and with her eyes filled with tears, Carol made a mistake behind the wheel. It resulted in her hitting hit the front bumper and grill of an SUV parked in the street. The SUV belonged to our neighbor, Johnny Boyle.

The ensuing impact caused a loud "bang!" that I heard from the front stoop of our home. The kids gathered across the street from me heard it too, and curious to see what happened, began to move in the direction of the sound.

Now, what I have to write here is very important: *From their original position and location, none of the children in the street intersection could have seen any more of what had happened further down the curved street than I had. A brick column on the porch of our house obscured my own view, so I didn't know what had happened myself.*

But as the kids milled about and started looking in a particular direction, I too went partway down our front steps to see what had caused the loud bang and what the kids were only now looking at. As I turned my head to look down the street, I saw Carol driving off.

I realized she must have hit something with the car. *And oh my goodness, to this day I wished she had just stayed put.*

She did not. Completely agitated, totally thrown, and frazzled, Carol told me later how hitting the SUV had pretty much unhinged her. She hopped out of our car briefly and glanced over at the SUV to see if there was any damage. She didn't see anything obvious, but did feel a small bit of relief upon recognizing the SUV as Johnny Boyle's. Since it belonged to her neighbor living right next door, it should be easy to handle any damage later on.

So thinking that any damage to the SUV — if there was any — must be very slight since she hadn't spotted any, Carol slipped back into our car and drove off to escape the kids, the possibility of even more taunting, and our neighborhood.

How sad I find her reaction to be that our neighborhood, and by extension our home, wasn't a place from which my wife could derive comfort and peace. The place that was supposed to be my wife's refuge...was not.

Carol's reaction obviously wasn't the right choice. But all Carol's mind was fixated on was her personal need to escape the taunting, settle her nerves, and find herself some peace again.

Her choice would come back to haunt her.

The Immediate Aftermath

The Fabuloso Restaurant, located on Keathley Boulevard about a mile from our home, was a quaint place with old-world charm. It was a place where Carol could relax, since she had been there several times before with friends after yoga class. So while Carol sat there sipping on some wine to settle her nerves, all hell was breaking loose in our neighborhood.

Someone had called the cops; within minutes of Carol's departure, three cop cars descended on the intersection. Several police officers hopped out to look at the front bumper of Johnny's SUV, make notes, and take photographs of the damage found on it.

Then, they began taking statements from several neighbors, mostly the kids. For once, several of their parents attended; they had come out of their homes because of all the cop cars on the street.

While everyone must have been wondering what had just gone down, only Carol and Willie White actually knew. Neither the basketball–playing kids nor I had been in a spot to witness the actual encounter between Willie and Carol.

When questioned, I told the police officer exactly what I had observed, and what I saw the kids doing. I told the officers about the kids harassing my wife, and about one of them making a Nazi party salute when she had left our home moments before.

One of the officers asked me in a calm, reasonable tone, "Where is your wife, so we can question her?"

No alarm bells went off in my brain at the thought of them going to speak to my wife: Their attitude suggested that they considered the incident a routine matter, and since I had provided them with the facts — including what had caused Carol's upset and therefore erratic driving — I did not doubt that the collision would be handled by our insurance company. Surely, the officers just needed to document what happened as best they could so the insurance agent could take it straight from their report.

Never did they give me any indication that they intended to arrest my wife over the matter.

I tried to call Carol on her cell phone so she could come home and speak to the officers here, but with all the upset she had endured, she had left it behind at home. So she couldn't answer my call.

The officers pressed me as to where she might have gone, and I gave them my best guess: "The Fabuloso Restaurant, since it's close and she's been there before."

As the officers drove off, I turned and made a comment to Willie's father, William White. It went something like, "You know, I'm kind of glad that this incident happened before the situation between Carol and the kids gets totally out of control."

Mr. White said nothing back; he just looked at me, then walked off. Odie Odom, overhearing me, just gave me a strange look.

I went back inside my home. *What an evening this was turning out to be!*

Arrested! (Who, Me?)

Note to the reader: At the recounting of those instances that follow where I was not present but my wife was, I am informing you as to what happened based upon what Carol can recall about those occurrences.

As Carol drank a glass of wine to settle her nerves, four or five stern-looking police officers stormed into the restaurant and came to her table shortly after six p.m.

"Are you Mrs. Clark-Brakke?" one of them asked. After my wife nodded in the affirmative, he said, "Okay, you'll have to come with us."

Carol was completely bewildered. "What?" she questioned. "What is this all about?"

One of the officers answered with, "You're under arrest. You have to come with us." Then he mumbled something she couldn't understand.

Carol felt foolish, dumbfounded, and embarrassed, too. The other diners were all looking at her, and she didn't have the slightest idea as to what was going on!

"No," she protested. "I don't know what this is all about. I won't go with you. You have the wrong person!"

Around this point, some of the police officers put their hands on her, twisting one of her arms up behind her, pulling her out of her chair, and handcuffing her.

Carol lost it, and began kicking and screaming in fear and horror.

As she struggled with the officers, the men dragged my wife out of the restaurant, and pushed her into a squad car.

Carol told me she yelled, "No, no! Why are you doing this? And where are you taking me?" But the officers didn't try to answer, question, or explain any of it to her.

Once Carol was in the squad car, one of the officers got behind the wheel of the car, and sped off.

A few minutes later, Carol was standing in front of an officer on duty at the Detective Division Offices. When she tried again to ask what it was all about, the officer glared at her with a hostile look, and brushed off her question.

Carol remained flummoxed: *What had she done to deserve this treatment? What had someone said about her, and who was it? What was she here for? Did she resemble a burglar? A murderer? What on earth was she here for, and why would no one give her the courtesy of telling her?* It was as if these officers were…in collusion against her!

Never in her entire life had Carol been in trouble with the law. She had never been treated this way. But there seemed to be nothing she could do about it.

The officer went about the business of booking her. He recorded her name and personal information. Then he pushed a fingerprinting card and ink box towards her.

"Just put the tips of each finger on the ink pad, and then place your print in the box for that finger on the card," he said.

Carol complied. Quietly. While in shock.

Then, still without informing her of the charges against her, two of the officers who had brought her to the police station escorted her somewhat forcibly through a door with bars on it into a holding cell.

The door swung shut, and Carol was alone. *In a cell!*

Carol started frantically thinking, *if it was me, and not a case of mistaken identity, what did I do? What could I possibly have done that was so awful that I am sitting here locked in a jail cell?*

She thought back over the events of the day but could think of nothing that stood out other than the real horror of being on the receiving end…of Nazi taunts and a Nazi salute, time and time again.

But how could that be it? Willie had insulted her, and even infuriated her as she drove past him, but what had she *done to him? Nothing. She hadn't done anything to him. So that couldn't be it.*

For a brief second, the thought that she had hit Johnny's SUV flitted through her head.

No, Carol immediately corrected herself, *that couldn't be it. I didn't see any damage.*

Nothing made sense.

Carol put her head down in her hands and began to moan out loud.

What a nightmare.

Happy birthday to me.

"Criminal Mischief"…. "Aggravated Assault?"

While Carol sat alone in a holding cell, detectives were interviewing Carol's two "victims" — as the charges lodged against Carol were for criminal mischief and aggravated assault.

There was twelve-year-old Willie White, the neighbor boy (and son of Tina) who often shot baskets or skateboarded out on the street. And there was Johnny Boyle, the owner of the SUV Carol inadvertently damaged before driving away.

Willie and Johnny each sat down with one of the officers in the interview room to give statements about what they claimed occurred.

A little later, Brody Odom and his 12-year old son Odie arrived too; they were similarly interviewed.

Carol never saw any of these individuals while she was in the holding cell. But they all said they saw her and heard her anguished moans emanating from her cell.

Carol knew she was groaning aloud. She was undone: She felt pure panic, unfettered worry, complete fear.

Nothing made sense: How could this be happening? How dare they do this to her? What did she do? All her life, she'd felt able to cope with tough situations, but now she felt helpless... and totally vulnerable. At the mercy of people who didn't have the decency to tell her what she had done; what she was in for.

That's right. Willie didn't tell the detectives anything about the fact that Carol had hit Johnny's car because she was upset and trying to get away from the kids who had been tormenting her with name-calling and Nazi salutes.

No.

Willie claimed Carol had tried to run him over.

That's right. That's what he told the detectives.

According to Willie, Carol didn't succeed in hitting him only because he was able to jump out of the way. And it was when she chased after him in reverse to attempt to hit him *again* that she hit Johnny's car — then drove away.

To this day, Carol and I aren't sure why a young boy like this would make up an enormity of a story that could derail a person's life.

Did Willie think he would get into trouble because of his taunting? Maybe.

Did he simply... hate Carol, because she had complained about where and how he played with the other neighborhood kids? Maybe.

Or... did the story he spun originate out of Willie's own desperate need for attention and connection in the face of his parents' divorce?

The last theory offers the only possible motivation Carol and I could come up with for the story he chose to spin.

Unfortunately, to the officers it appeared that Willie was telling the truth. And my wife and I both recognize that Carol's fear and resistance when the officers appeared out of nowhere at Fabuloso Restaurant had not helped correct their already-formed but wrong impression of her.

Two officers arrived to escort Carol — *in handcuffs* — to the Podleski County Regional Jail. They put her in a small jail cell with a narrow cot, toilet, and washbasin. When some female guards asked Carol to strip and take a shower, she refused. To their credit, they didn't force her. They turned and left, simply locking the door of the cell behind them.

As Carol sat in the cell in stunned silence, an officer called me to reassure me: "We've got Carol, and she's perfectly safe. You can pick her up if you dial this number to make the arrangements." Then he read off a phone number.

As I jotted down the number with shaking fingers, I remember thinking: *What had happened to Carol? Why did she need to be picked up? Why didn't she have our car? What had happened to her since I last saw her?*

I managed to ask the officer where our car was before he signed off. He told me it was behind the Fabuloso Restaurant.

Worriedly, I called the phone number the officer had given me. It's impossible to describe, in writing, my reaction when I discovered this was the number of someone at the county jail.

My wife Carol was in jail? For what? Why? What had happened to her after she left? I had to get her out of there as quickly as possible!

I found out that to bail Carol out, I had to get in touch with a bail bondsman. So I called one, only to be told that what I would have to pay is, "...10% of the total fee of bond, which is to assure her [Carol's] appearance in court."

I hung up, and nervously searched around for my checkbook. I hurriedly walked the mile or so to the restaurant to retrieve our car. Then I drove to meet the bail bondsman in front of the jail, as he had instructed.

After the heavy-set black bondsman paid the bail to the booking officer, an attendant brought Carol out from her cell so I could take her home.

She looked awful, her face pale, her hair messed. She was shaking nervously as she stood beside the attendant.

"You're free to go now," the attendant said, guiding her towards me.

Tentatively, she stepped towards me, as if still bewildered by everything that had happened to her. We hugged intensely.

The bail bondsman told us, "As long as she appears for her hearings, there will be no more charges. The bail is just to make sure she shows up in court, as it's scheduled." Then he gave us his address and told us to meet him there to take care of some further details.

Carol was in no condition to do more than smile weakly at me, so I helped her walk to the car.

As we drove off, Carol began to weep. She was in no condition to tell me what happened, and the truth was, she didn't know! Not only had she not been read her rights, she hadn't been questioned by the police even! *(Only later did I learn that Willie White had claimed my wife tried to run him over — which is what led to her arrest.)*

At the bail bondsman's office, there were more papers to sign. He emphasized too the importance of my making sure that Carol attended every hearing while out on bail; otherwise, her bail would be revoked.

"Do you understand?" he asked Carol.

"Yes," she said, nodding weakly. "I'll be there."

I then asked the bail bondsman if he had any suggestion for a lawyer, and he recommended John Guildenstern.

"He's very well respected in the black community," the bondsman told me.

Carol and I truly appreciated receiving this personal recommendation, as we had absolutely no experience in matters of a criminal nature.

The Next Twenty-Four Hours

The next twenty-four hours at home after Carol's arrest did not go well.

First: Carol was so wound up from her ordeal that, understandably, for the whole night, she couldn't sleep.

Second: We got up the next morning, only to stumble upon a brief article in our local newspaper.

The article clued us in to the enormity of the situation we as a family now faced.

The article indicated that Willie told police that Carol: a). tried to hit him with her car at first; b). tried to hit his feet when she opened her car door to get out; and c). attempted to hit him again by flooring the car in reverse — (which is when she ended up hitting Johnny's SUV).

No wonder the police had treated Carol they way that had...

But it was not until Carol and I read that newspaper article that we had an understanding of what the police had been told, because, at the risk of being repetitive, she had never been informed as to the charges against her. Nor had the police ever questioned her about the matter!

It seemed like the police had already chosen a side to take — something they should never do. *Innocent until proven guilty — right?*

From reading the article in the paper, it became clear to both Carol and me that not only were the authorities predisposed to believe Willie, but also that now the whole neighborhood undoubtedly was going to mobilize against us.

Feeling defenseless against what would become a combined attack, Carol wanted to look into getting a lawyer right away. So that very morning we went straight to John Guildenstern's office, to see if he would take on Carol's case. We showed him the article in the paper, and he seemed intrigued by Carol's situation. He asked her a number of questions, yet despite her offering thorough and satisfactory answers, he did not immediately agree to represent her. But Carol desperately felt she needed a lawyer right away, and pressed him to agree to represent her. Finally, he said he would.

I had misgivings. The physical state of the man's office gave me no confidence in Guildenstern. His office was a total mess: papers strewn everywhere and there was even a toppled-over grocery-shopping cart by one wall! I didn't see how any lawyer could be successful surrounded by that amount of disorganization.

Still, his agreement made Carol feel relieved. She had hope that her ordeal was mostly over, now that she had a lawyer who could right this insane wrong.

So we went back home. There, I told Carol she needed to tell Johnny about the crash, apologize, and offer to pay for any damages. She went over there and tried to do so, but Johnny reacted strangely, continuing to bag leaves and ignoring her.

At that time, we did not know that Johnny had already filed charges against her.

CHAPTER 3: FROM BAD TO WORSE

A few days later, a nicely dressed young woman rang our doorbell and asked for Carol. After I got my wife, she handed Carol a document addressed to her.

"I'm so sorry to have to give this to you," she said, a sheepish look on her face.

"What are these for?" Carol asked, her voice quavering.

"I'm afraid you'd better get yourselves a lawyer," the woman said softly before she headed to her car, which she had parked down the block.

Carol gasped in dismay, as she looked at the papers, unable to catch her breath.

It was a petition from our neighbor Brody Odom to have Carol committed on the grounds she was mentally disturbed. In part, it said that Carol was, "…a clear and present danger to herself or others… cursing out children… cursing me [Brody Odom] out… accusing people of doing things when they are not present or couldn't have even done the things… attempted to run over a boy."

Brody was claiming Carol had tried to run Willie over. I couldn't believe the untruth of this accusation. Neither he nor his son Odie could have seen this happen! Brody wasn't even there. Also, I was witness to the fact that Odie was with the kids playing in front of Willie's house at the time, and that was located on a block that curved away from the scene of the actual incident. *Both the curve and our neighbor's new fence would have obscured the view of everyone playing over there!*

But since my neighbor had filed the petition, now we had to appear in court. The truth or falsity of the petition would be a subject for the court to decide.

We looked at the petition more closely, and noticed it was riddled with grammatical mistakes.

"What an ignoramus," I commented to Carol, trying to make light of the situation.

Despite my comment, I knew this was something we had to treat seriously. So, in light of the fact that I really didn't know anything about Brody Odom except that he lived next door, or what the LCSW after his signature meant, I decided to find out more about him. I Googled him — only to discover he worked at the same place where Carol had recently started going for counseling right after being arrested!

I called the place, and made inquiries. I learned "LCSW" stood for "licensed clinical social worker," and that Brody Odom had graduated from the University of East Kansas at Big Pebble, and was employed by my own institution. I was shocked to discover he had his Master's Degree, since his writing and typing ability was so poor, as shown in the petition.

It truly bothered me that this man was using his knowledge of the mental health and justice systems as a social worker to institute a vendetta against a neighbor who wasn't familiar with the process or systems. I called our lawyer, John Guildenstern, to ask what to do.

He didn't seem terribly concerned: "Don't worry," he assured us. "This petition is just a frivolous request, and it'll never be granted by a judge."

Did he just figure that he could object to the petition a few times, ask that it be thrown out, and that would be that?

We told Guildenstern we were eager to give our side of the events and argue back against the false charges. *He advised Carol and me not to testify*: "You shouldn't say anything," he told us firmly. "I'm sure this petition is just a ploy to reveal evidence that might be used against Carol in the aggravated assault case. Anything you say in this hearing could be used against you, so it's better to remain silent."

Guildenstern was so sure of himself — and not knowing any better, we trusted him and went along with what he said. Carol worried a little about doing so, but I reminded her that Guildenstern was very confident about the matter. I was certain he must be right because no lawyer worth his or her salt would set us up for a fall without preparing us for the possibility of a fall, and after all, Guildenstern hadn't even bothered to tell us what to expect if he was wrong. He was THAT confident. Guildenstern believed he knew what he was talking about and could convince the judge to dismiss the petition. So he never even bothered to question us to help him prepare an aggressive defense. He also did not coach us on how to handle it if we heard a lie in court in terms of others' testimony.

His erroneous belief that a judge would never grant the request, and our naïve support of and faith in him as our lawyer, would be our undoing.

The Mental Health Hearing

The hearing (because it was an issue of mental health) was held at the state hospital about two weeks later.

Judge Esther Brinkley, a Judge for one of the Circuit Courts in East Kansas, presided at this Podleski County Circuit Court proceeding, along with a Prosecuting Attorney, as required by a Section 5 proceeding for an involuntary commitment. Brody and Odie Odom were there to provide their testimony on behalf of the State.

Carol sat nervously in the room beside Guildenstern. She was shaking a little as she tried to keep control. I sat by myself in the very back of the courtroom.

The judge began by asking the prosecutor what testimony she expected to put on, and the prosecutor replied that she had Brody and Odie Odom with her to testify. Then she asked Mr. Guildenstern if Carol was planning to testify.

"No, Your Honor," Guildenstern replied. "There's a criminal charge pending, and I've advised her of her rights."

"All right. She's not required to," the judge responded.

The judge then swore in Brody and his son, and asked them to testify alone in turn. After they each raised their right hands, they solemnly swore that the testimony they were going to give "…will be the truth, the whole truth, and nothing but the truth, so help you God."

Odie was excused, and Brody Odom was first to testify.

He explained that he had been next-door neighbors with Carol for about one year, and that as a licensed clinical social worker for the Department of Psychiatry of the University of East Kansas Medical Sciences, he had "…been working with mental illness for fifteen-plus years." He also offered that he had a master's degree in social work.

Guildenstern immediately challenged whether Odom was being called as an "expert witness" or a "lay witness." So the judge agreed that Odom could only testify as a neighbor and witness to what he had seen, and not as a mental health expert.

However, it remains my opinion that the fact that he provided his professional experience upon taking the stand gave him added authority about mental illness in the eyes of the judge, and his testimony added weight.

Brody then testified that he had seen a worrisome pattern of behavior from Carol that amounted to "…increasing paranoia and aggression… verbal insults, with Carol cursing at small children, myself, other neighbors." He also said that Carol was making "paranoid accusations based on misidentifications."

The evidence Brody provided for this?

"She told me my son was out in front of her house and he jumped in front of her car on a skateboard, when I knew he was three blocks over inside somebody else's house."

When John Guildenstern complained to the judge that this statement was based on hearsay, the judge had to admonish Brody to only talk about what he observed.

Brody went on and on, citing examples of what he believed to be "mentally ill and accusatory" behavior on Carol's part, including, "I've seen her call the police on numerous occasions… She called the police when some neighbor children knocked gravel off a stone wall. It probably added up to two ounces of gravel."

I winced when I heard this. He was referring to when the neighborhood boys were defacing the wall of the black family in our neighborhood. Well, it wasn't a few chips! They had hacked out a large piece of stone out of the neighbor's wall, and we had pictures of that damage. (Too bad we did not have those pictures in court.) In no way was the damage something that amounted only to small chips. Besides, neighbors aren't being friendly if they ruin something that has taken a neighbor considerable expense to have constructed? Such an incident is an example of young children misbehaving — or children turning out the wrong way in their adolescent and teen years.

As Brody, and then his son Odie, went to misrepresent the actual occurrences on the stand, I could observe my wife repeatedly learning over to Guildenstern to dispute the father-and-son-team's version of events (something I confirmed with her later, since I could not hear her words from where I was sitting at the time). I even passed occasional notes to our lawyer, advising him to object to some of this testimony myself, since some of what I heard was so egregiously incorrect and wrong.

But Guildenstern just nodded as if to say, "I heard your suggestions," and then did nothing to object. Nor did he later seek to show on cross-examination that Brody or Odie could not be telling the truth.

I still cannot figure out why. *I had to guess Guildenstern must have decided in advance not to aggressively cross-examine the witnesses simply because he assumed the judge would just toss out the petition regardless. Or… might something else be going on? As of this writing, and to this day, I do not really know. (Nor does Carol.)*

The result was that Brody and Odie were able to offer up countless accusations, nearly all of which went unopposed by our attorney.

Brody claimed to see my wife, "…physically approach children that are not hers, [by] going out of her property across the street, pointing fingers and cursing them. Young children." When asked by the judge what it was that my wife supposedly said, he claimed she had said, "You're a fucking asshole," to kids as young as seven!

How ironic that the very terminology he used to damage Carol was the exact vocabulary he had used to disparage her on occasion!

Plus Brody testified that while he was sitting on his front stoop one day with a small group of people, Carol physically approached Odie on the street. He said Odie was simply sitting on the back of their car watching some other kids play football. He claimed, "…she was screaming at him [Odie], yelling at him, cursing him, [and] telling him that he was harassing her in some way when he was looking in a different direction… [She was pointing her finger in his face, and he [Odie] was scared and backed up and stumbled and fell. I had to intervene at that point."

As Carol confirmed to me later, it was another lie. *Ironic again* that *not only was Brody's statement untrue, it was* Brody *who had pointed his finger at Carol. He had stepped forward, so close that it was an invasion of Carol's personal space and threatened to hit her.*

Brody claimed the children had done nothing to provoke her. They were, he said, "simply playing basketball, riding scooters and bicycles, throwing Frisbees" and "none of this was in her yard."

Brody also described how Carol approached a young woman who was pregnant "…in a very threatening and hostile, terrifying manner… [Carol] put her finger in her face and said… 'You're going to have a baby, I'm going to be there.'" Brody then said that Carol's tone of voice as she said these words was "…very agitated, hostile, and just frightening to me."

As Carol told me later, she never said this to the woman in question, or put her finger in anyone's face. In fact, Carol had been friendly with this woman until the lady's husband (Butler) called her a "Nazi" in front of the kids — at which point, Carol stopped having any social interactions with her.

Carol shook upon hearing these falsehoods, and felt horrible about having to remain silent in her chair, unable to testify and correct all the lies. But all she could do was sit and listen, and try quietly to tell her lawyer what had truly happened in each instance. But since our lawyer had deemed that it would be better for my wife to remain silent and not "give away" any information that might be used against her in the criminal case, Carol now was unable to correct the falsehoods and misinformation in court — unless our lawyer did it for her.

Any confidence Carol had regarding the outcome of this hearing quickly started unraveling. She started thinking: *But what about* this *case? What if this hearing goes against me? What if Guildenstern's confidence that the judge would quickly throw out this frivolous claim of mental illness is misplaced? It certainly doesn't seem like the judge is treating this case as a frivolous one.*

Damning "testimony" against Carol continued. On and on. Brody described her as acting like a caged animal when he had gone to the Big Pebble Police Station to give a statement to the police on the day of Carol's birthday. As Brody described it, he saw her in handcuffs escorted by the police into a back interior room, and then heard her "...screaming and wailing in rather bizarre wail-like sounds... It really sounded like nothing I've ever heard come out of a human being before, but it sounded like an animal being tortured or a... rather ghost-like sound. And I heard... bizarre moaning and I heard her accuse... a black police officer of being in the KKK, being a Nazi."

Later on, Carol acknowledged to me that she might have sounded a bit like a tortured animal in her holding cell that evening, since indeed she was agitated — even hysterical — about being arrested without knowing why. So she had sat there in the cell crying, sobbing, and moaning out loud. But she certainly never had accused a "black officer" of being in the KKK or of being a Nazi!

The prosecutor asked if Brody had any contact with Carol in the weeks since.

Brody said he had not, and that when he looked over at our house, "...The only thing I've seen is that video cameras have been mounted in her front windows, and... the 'record' lights [were] on."

When Brody mentioned this, I shifted in my seat uncomfortably. I had thought it might be a good idea to start recording the dangerous antics in the intersection, in case this might prove helpful to our lawyer as he built our case. But in the light of Brody's testimony, I grew uncomfortably aware that my brilliant idea for evidence to support our case and Carol's actions might have not been so brilliant after all!

Then Brody noted that he had seen Carol staring out of a window as part of an escalating pattern of her looking out the window: "Since we've moved in, I've seen her spending up to five hours of staring out the window at the children as they play in a rather bizarre fixed state of just staring."

Carol told me that as Brody spoke about this in the hospital's courtroom, she thought back to the times she had looked out of the windows of our home: *Sure, I've gazed out from time to time. Who hasn't looked out the window of their homes to admire the yard or check out what's going on in the neighborhood when they hearing yelling, for example? But for five hours at a time? No, never. Besides, how could Brody testify about making this observation if he himself wasn't sitting or standing there watching himself for five hours straight at a time? Why is no one challenging him on this point?*

Sadly, Guildenstern's cross-examination of Brody proved perfunctory. And Brody denied ever hearing the neighborhood kids yell at my wife, call her a Nazi, or give her a Nazi salute. He did acknowledge that Carol complained about the rim of the basketball net overhanging the street, and that a person might expect her to be upset after being arrested and hauled off to the police station.

Guildenstern never tried to get Brody to be more specific about the odd or threatening behavior he claimed he observed in Carol so that he might poke holes in the claims. Guildenstern's softball questions only served to leave the impression that Brody had testified truthfully in support of his petition to declare Carol mentally ill and have her involuntarily committed for a week of observation.

The "evidence" continued to mount, and go unchallenged as to its veracity.

Twelve-year-old Odie Odom was summoned and he started by describing the language he supposedly heard Carol use. "She cusses… like a-hole and stuff."

Then, Odie described some of the aggressive things he claimed Carol did. "Sometimes when I'm playing outside, she comes out and just hollers at some of the neighborhood kids that live out there where we live down the street… I was on my car, and she just came out and she was just yelling and stuff."

According to Odie, he didn't do anything to make Carol angry, although he said sometimes a football he was throwing would land in her yard, and he would go get it. Odie testified he never tried to do anything to make her angry, although some of his friends did, and he did nothing to provoke Carol when she pointed a finger at him about four weeks ago. Even worse, Odie claimed Carol would act in an aggressive way once or twice a week.

Then Odie gave his version about what happened that October day to support his friend's claim she had tried to run him over: "My friend was skateboarding down the road towards the park, and she was backing out of the driveway and tried to run over him. He jumped out of the way and then she backed up the hill. Then I guess she tried to back over him again, but she missed him, and he got out of the way."

Again, I was aghast at what was occurring in the court this day. I had been an observer that day as well, so I knew perfectly well this boy could not have seen what he claimed. *What was motivating this young man to lie like this?*

As he had done with the boy's father, Guildenstern did nothing in his cross-examination to undermine Odie's testimony. To my consternation, he didn't ask about where Odie claimed he was when he saw this, for this would have shown the boy couldn't have seen what he said he did! Nor did Guildenstern seek to show that the incident itself couldn't have happened as described.

In the cross-examination, Guildenstern did bring up the fact that Carol had complained to Odie and others that they shouldn't play in that particular intersection because it was dangerous. And when Guildenstern asked Odie about the complaints of the neighborhood kids about Carol's behavior, it ended up reinforcing the prosecution's case against Carol!

Specifically, Odie responded to our attorney's question with answers like, "Willie… don't call her 'Nazi.' He calls her a 'German lady'… He doesn't yell [at her]. He just says, 'Stop looking at us out your window' and stuff like that, because she's always looking out her window at us… She just keeps hovering around her window every day… like she's trying to stalk us, and that gets us freaked out."

When asking Odie about the car incident, Guildenstern did nothing to demonstrate that Odie couldn't have seen what he claimed. I was horrified he didn't use any diagrams to show where Odie was positioned while Carol was supposedly driving at Willie, reversing her car, and driving towards him again. And since Guildenstern had gotten Carol to agree not to testify, she couldn't refute Odie's claim that she had aimed her car at Willie.

Carol and I faced a "he said, she said" kind of scenario — except that our lawyer had removed any possibility of "she said."

After his cross-examination of Odie, Guildenstern did make one last attempt to dismiss the petition. He asked to address the court, and weakly offered, "Your Honor, I think probably technically I would move to dismiss, because the prosecutor hasn't met her burden."

Guildenstern was referring to the burden of proof for bringing a case before a judge, which in a civil case such as this is low. *The prosecutor must merely show at a petition hearing that there's sufficient evidence to move forward and accept the petition.* But nothing in the hearing had contradicted the "eyewitness testimony" of Brody or Odie! So there *was* enough evidence.

When Guildenstern sat down, it was up to the judge to decide for, or against, the petition.

Judge Brinkley simply said, "Overruled... And the petition is granted."

At first, we didn't know what this meant, except that it didn't sound good for us.

Here, Guildenstern rose to his feet and questioned the judge as to why she was granting the petition. Her response was, "I believe that she [Carol] has a mental illness that poses a threat of harm to others."

Like a sledgehammer on our brains, the words "mental illness" hit Carol and me. *Mentally ill? If Carol were mentally ill, I would have known it after all our years of marriage. It was so out of proportion, so over the top, for the Odoms (and Willie) to make these claims because Carol protested a few times about the kids playing in the street, something that was not only noisy and disruptive, but dangerous.*

Now ill-intentioned neighbors had manipulated the court with their lies — and neither Carol nor I knew what was in store for her in the future. Our lives had been placed in the hands of neighbors who wanted to toy with us, or even hated us; we didn't know which.

But our lives were at someone else's mercy now.

Guildenstern asked the judge to agree that the findings of the court hearing and anything Carol did to cooperate during her involuntary commitment and evaluation be treated as "privileged" (kept in confidence) because she was facing a criminal charge. But Judge Brinkley said she had no ability to do anything, because, "the person who's going to make the decision about whether privilege applies is whoever the judge is who has the criminal case."

Still, she sought to reassure us by adding that she assumed that, "Anything Carol says [during the evaluation process] will be for the purpose of treatment and, therefore, will be covered by the client's right of privilege." However, she couldn't make any determination about it herself.

With that, the hearing was over.

We had lost the case and most certainly for two reasons: a) because Guildenstern, mistakenly thinking the petition would be considered "frivolous," came to court unprepared to fight back with a strong cross-examination; and b) thinking that whatever Carol or I might say on the stand might prove harmful to the criminal case against Carol, our lawyer refused to put Carol and/or me on the stand to offer our version of events, leaving us no chance to expose and contradict any untruthful testimony offered against her.

What Could Be Next?

We were ushered to another room at the State Hospital for some sort of interview. I was allowed to accompany Carol, and as I walked beside her, I thought she looked more depressed and defeated than ever. Her hands and body shook nervously, and her eyes were glazed from the tears welling up in them. "We'll fight this," I assured her.

But like her, I felt a sense of grim hopelessness. For now, not only were the police, prosecutor, and court aligned against us based on our neighbors' false accusations and testimony, but we had a lawyer who didn't seem up to the task of properly defending us.

Now, Carol and I could have used some legal guidance or some support as we moved on to whatever was in store, but Guildenstern informed us, "I have to go." Explaining that he had some other obligation, he left without telling us anything further about what to expect.

I was furious. Not only had Guildenstern led us to believe we would prevail at the hearing, but his decision not to let us testify and his inept defense had doomed Carol to a period in a mental hospital! And now there was another betrayal: *Not only had he not told us previously what would happen if we lost at the hearing, but he had just vanished on us, **again without telling us what would happen next!***

The interview that ensued in another room turned out to involve both Carol and me, and it was designed to gather the necessary information for admitting Carol to the hospital. Those conducting the interview asked us for such information as Carol's age and insurance.

Then, the intake officer told us that they would take Carol in a van to Lutheran Hospital's psych ward.

What? Now? Already? It wasn't going to be in the future?

Carol and I were dumbfounded.

The unexpected shocks just kept coming. Over and over again. We had never been through a process like this, and Carol and I were like two deer caught in the headlights of an accelerating car.

Then, looking at me, the officer added in soft, calm tone, "I'm sorry, sir, that you won't be able to come with us in the van. But you can follow us in your car."

"W-why not?" was all I managed to utter as my wife's face grew white with fear.

"Because," he said, "we'll be admitting Carol, and you will need a way to get back to your home [once that happens]."

That made sense, so Carol and I didn't protest. We just did as directed — separately, but very glumly.

I followed the van in my car for about three miles down a freeway. Soon after our vehicles exited, the van pulled up to a huge, boxy building. It looked like a fortress — and it would become one for Carol.

Ahead of me, and guided by two officers on either side of her, Carol walked slowly, like a zombie, into the hospital. I parked quickly, and met them upstairs a few minutes later.

CHAPTER 4: COMMITTED!

Being Admitted

After offering us a brief welcome, the receptionist got down to business: "We just ask that you follow all our rules, and we'll have some tests to give you. Please hand over your personal belongings, ma'am; we'll take care of them for you at the front desk. There's a hospital gown for you to wear once you're admitted."

Carol gazed at the receptionist in stony silence. My guess is that not only was she still trying to process what had just been said to her, but she was unwilling to accept what was about to happen to her. Finally, she responded with, "No, I won't. I won't hand over my personal belongings to you."

"Please, you have to do this," the receptionist insisted.

"No. I don't want to give you anything. I don't want to be here."

The receptionist reiterated, "Please, we just need you to give us your personal belongings. That means your purse, your outer clothing, and the jewelry you are wearing. You can't hold onto anything sharp, and also no cell phone or cosmetics."

Repeatedly Carol refused as the receptionist repeated her directives. In fact, she became more and more hysterical. She was in real agony.

"No, I won't hand over anything. I don't belong here!" Carol declared adamantly. Then she began crying, exhausted and frightened over what might happen next.

I tried to intercede and tell the receptionist that she should try to calm Carol down first instead of arguing with her. It was no use: This encounter had already escalated into a full-blown confrontation.

"You can't do this! You can't take my property," Carol objected, her voice getting louder and louder. "Nobody can commit me against my will. You're violating my civil rights. I want to go home. I don't want to be here. Take me home *now!*"

The commotion had reached the ears of others, and a nurse came over to glare at Carol with an icy stare. "If you don't shut up right now, we'll put you with the criminally insane around the corner, and that will teach you," she enunciated clearly, pointing down the hall to a corner sign that said, "Criminally insane ward."

Carol hesitated, looking lost and uncertain.

"Please, go ahead. Do what they want," I implored. "It'll be easier for you."

I don't know if it was my voice of reason, the nurse's threat, or my wife's evident exhaustion that prevailed, but Carol finally acquiesced very dejectedly. "Okay. Whatever you want. Whatever you say."

As she handed over her jewelry and belongings, the receptionist promised to put them in a safe for her.

Then, another nurse came over to get Carol and lead her down the corridor to her new quarters. I wasn't allowed to go with her, so I kissed her and stood by the desk waving a goodbye at her.

Checked-In

Carol waved back sadly, then walked silently away with the nurse.

The nurse led Carol into a dimly lit windowless room; it housed a bed with a green hospital gown on it, a night table, and nothing else. To Carol, the room felt like a prison cell, for it offered only a cement floor under her feet.

After Carol obediently donned the hospital gown, she dropped onto the bed and fell asleep. The day's trauma had wiped her out completely.

Around 11 p.m., a sudden, unexpected knock on Carol's door woke her from a dead sleep. Groggily, she opened her eyes. In the darkness, she spied the vague outline of a being with a blue light blinking from the left ear. The unanticipated apparition scared her. It seemed like some alien was now her captor.

Carol sat up straight in bed and asked, "Who are you? Why are you here?"

A muffled voice from the doorway said, "I'm here to talk to you about what brought you here."

Not wanting to talk to anyone about anything right now, and wanting just to go to sleep, Carol spat back, "I really don't know why I'm here, and I don't want to talk about it now!"

With that, Carol dropped her head back on the pillow and turned away from this strange person.

"Okay, we'll talk about this later," the person said.

Then, the individual shut the door and was gone. Friday was over, but it certainly hadn't been any TGIF.

A New Day

Carol woke up shortly before eight a.m. Saturday to an announcement on the intercom: "Breakfast — 8 a.m."

The feeling of being totally alone and vulnerable hit her, although later Carol would learn she was being watched continually. She looked around her; the starkness of her small room with only a bed and nightstand reminded her that she desperately didn't want to be here.

Carol soon left her room and spied a multi-level cart containing breakfast sitting in the hallway. She found the tray with her name on it, and a nurse standing nearby told her to take it to a designated meal area next to the main socializing area.

"How long do I have for breakfast?" Carol inquired.

"An hour," the nurse said. "Then at 9:15 a.m., you need to go to a 'Group Session.' You'll hear it announced on the intercom."

"I don't want to go," Carol said. "I shouldn't be here."

But the nurse insisted: "If you keep carrying on like this, they'll just keep you here longer."

That registered with Carol, and she managed to convince herself to comply. She felt awful but knew that agonizing all day wouldn't help. She'd better try to put on an act and do what they wanted. She got dressed.

Inside the dining area, Carol joined a small group and found them eager to talk, although mostly everyone complained about how terrible the food tasted and how miserable they felt.

After breakfast, Carol went to the nurse's station with a few requests, since patients had to go here whenever they wanted something.

"I need some things now," she told the nurse on duty. "Some towels and wash clothes. I'd also like a toothbrush and tooth paste."

"I don't know," said the nurse. "I'll have to see what I can do. I'll bring you what I can in a little while."

This nurse didn't realize I had come back the evening before to leave some toiletries and reading materials for my wife with the receptionist.

Returning to her room, Carol sat back down on the bed, trying to hold back the tears.

Everything around her seemed so controlled, so precise, everything regulated by the clock. Yet inside she felt a sense of rising chaos, like a giant wave coming up out of the ocean to engulf her. She needed to stay firm, she told herself. She needed to hold onto her churning emotions to ride out the wave.

Minutes later, there was an announcement: "The groups are starting now. Please go to the conference room to meet your group."

Carol asked a nurse in the hallway, "What are the groups about?"

"They are where you discuss your issues and learn coping skills," the nurse replied.

She led Carol into a conference room with a dozen other patients, some in everyday clothes, others still in their gowns. They sat in a circle along with a counselor-facilitator wearing a suit.

"Welcome, Carol," the group facilitator said, pointing to one of the empty folding chairs. "We're glad to have you with us."

The group session began with the patients introducing themselves by their first names and saying why they were there.

"Hello, I'm Jerry. And I have a problem with controlling my anger."

"Hi, I'm Susan. I came here because I punched out my husband. I got tired of him calling me names.

"Hi, I'm Barbara. I'm here because I'm bipolar. I am in my manic phase at present."

"Hi, I'm Jack. I got hooked on pain killers, and that's why I almost got fired from my job."

It was Carol's turn.

"Hi, I'm Carol. I was brought here against my will. I was involuntarily committed to this place, which is a terrible thing. It's very different from all those of you who came here voluntarily, because you knew you needed help." She confided how grief stricken she was.

"Yes, that is unfortunate," the counselor agreed. "But maybe we can still help you in the group. Please feel welcome here, and feel free to share what you want."

As the session continued, Carol felt her spirits lifting. *It felt good to be with others who seemed to understand what she was going through, since they had their own problems to deal with.*

At the end of the session, Carol walked towards the door smiling for the first time since her arrival. She felt somehow lighter and freer, as if she had released some of her burdens to the group.

On the way back to her room, Carol was able to get some bathroom supplies— soap, lotion, powder, and deodorant —from the main desk. The head nurse noted this in the assessment history report, which would be part of the record to be submitted to a judge to determine Carol's state of mental health. Her note at this time was: Pt. [patient] came out of groups smiling and more pleasant. She requested soap, lotion, powder, and deodorant, which was given to her. Will continue to observe behavior. Will continue with the treatment plan.

Yet, even though Carol had left the group feeling better, this mood soon left her: When she reached her room, the oppressiveness of being alone in her small, stark room weighed on her. She broke out in a nervous sweat, and touched a button to call for a nurse.

When the nurse arrived, she refused Carol's request to give her some of her usual medicine to calm her nerves and lift her spirits. That's when Carol found out her nighttime visitor had been her new doctor, Doctor Kaczmarek (and that the blinking blue light on his ear had been a Bluetooth device!). By her not wanting to talk at that moment in the middle of the night to this unexpected and eerie-looking visitor, she would not be able to receive her usual medicines until her doctor spoke with her and approved it. But Dr. Kaczmarek wouldn't be making rounds again until his next visit... on Monday!

Carol couldn't help but protest: "I'm feeling so anxious! I can't handle all this without the medicine I normally get." (Carol had been on antidepressants and anti-anxiety medications for several years.)

"Well, then," the nurse said, "we do have something we can give you to relax you. We recommend you try some medication we can give to the patients."

Carol agreed, desperate to get something to help quell her growing anxiety.

The nurse gave her some sort of pill to swallow, and Carol did so.

The receptionist sent down the reading material I had brought her, but after an hour, Carol was feeling more anxious than ever. *Had the medicine not worked, or worn off already?* She headed to the nurse's station, crying and shaking.

"Please, I can't handle this," she implored. "I should never have been taken off my regular medication like this. The medication you gave me obviously isn't working, and I'm more upset than ever!"

A few nurses together sought to reassure Carol that everything would be okay, but when it didn't prove effective, one of the nurses came over with a glass of water and some pills in a little plastic cup.

Eagerly, Carol downed the pills, hoping for some relief. Somehow, the act of swallowing them, in conjunction with having the nurses around her felt soothing. Carol became a little calmer now.

The nurses relaxed as well, as if the crisis was averted.

"Would you like to talk about what you've been experiencing?" the nurse in charge asked.

And now Carol did; she felt like she had to let go and talk to someone to release the tension that had been building inside her.

"Yes, I do," said Carol. "I've been under a lot of stress lately. I have had a good life so far, but now I'm nervous about my upcoming hearing in front of a judge about the criminal assault charge and leaving the scene of an accident. I'm not sure what's going to happen. My accusers could make up anything — they have already — and if they are believed, I could end up in a mental hospital or prison for a very long time. So I'm very scared."

"Of course, you are," the nurse sympathized. "You have a lot to deal with."

Carol nodded and continued, "But at least I have the support of my husband and kids. That makes me feel a little better. My daughter lives in New Hampshire, and my son is in the Philippines doing outsourcing for an American business. But my son will return to the U.S. in a month, and my daughter will fly here to be with me during the hearing. I'm really glad to know they'll be here."

"That's wonderful," the nurse agreed. "Having your family support you is so important in challenging times like these."

Carol nodded, and the nurses continued to sit with her for a few minutes, giving her their support.

She got more support from her family when I arrived for a visit at two p.m.

Her First Visit

Patients on the ward were only allowed visitors twice a day for an hour after lunch and another hour in the evening, and I visited religiously.

I met with Carol in the dayroom, a large room filled with old furniture that looked like it came from the Salvation Army. This was the only room in the ward with windows, and although they couldn't be opened, at least there were no bars on them!

Once Carol saw me, she ran across the room to greet me, eager to see me and tell me what her time at the facility had been like. Mostly, we talked about what had happened to us and how we hoped everything would soon end, so we could go back to our normal life.

We had much to say, and our meeting seemed to be over far too soon.

"I'll come again later in the evening, and at the same time tomorrow," I reassured her.

Then, it was time to go. After giving Carol a quick kiss under the watchful eye of one of the nurses, I was off.

My visit had improved Carol's mood, and the nurse jotted down: 1400: Pt. quietly resting. Had a good visit with her husband. Her mood has improved, but she continues to voice a lot of frustration with being here on the unit. Will continue to provide support.

Adjusting

In her time spent in the ward, Carol experienced a variety of moods alternating between anger, despair, and depression. They hadn't yet gotten around to evaluating her psychologically.

Carol told me when she felt angry, she would sit on her new bed in her dreary room and dream about suing the Odoms for defamation, mental and emotional suffering, and malicious prosecution. Only that, she told me, could calm her sense of injustice, and eliminate her inner anger.

The nurses, meticulous in their observation and note-taking, made this note one time after Carol had been expressed her anger and frustration over the injustice of being placed her in the ward: 1) Risk for violence: Progressing. No violent behavior observed while the patient has been on the unit. 2) Coping slow to progress. The patient continues to be frustrated, angry, and speaks her mind regarding the doctor. She has not spoken of the incident that has placed her on this unit. Will continue to observe. Will continue to support.

Most of the time though, Carol's anger gave way to anxiety, desolation, and despair. The stark cement walls surrounding her in a prison-like room made Carol feel felt scared and alone. At these times, she was like a caged lion that had all the fight, vim, and vigor squeezed out of it. To deal with this, she had to ask for medicine to help her cope.

The nurses usually agreed, although when they gave Carol her pills they might ask a question like, "Have you had any auditory or visual hallucinations today?"

When they did, Carol would respond, "No, no, nothing like that. Just there are somewhat overwhelming feelings of anxiety, because I don't need to be here, shouldn't be here. And what they say about me isn't true: I've never been aggressive towards anyone, and I'm certainly not mentally ill."

As the days passed, Carol started to be able to relax a bit more during her time in the ward, though she continued to worry about her upcoming mental health evaluation and the pending court trial. She began to confide in the nurses on duty about these concerns.

"Don't worry," one nurse assured her. "You seem more relaxed and comfortable here now, so I'm sure you'll do fine."

Happily, the nurses became a solid form of support for Carol. As they observed her and her behavior, and as Carol spoke with them, the nurses came to believe in her and her story. I found this out one day when I came for a visit and spoke with some of the staff at the nursing station. When I said I was here to visit with Carol, one of the nurses spoke up.

"Carol told us the story about the neighbor's complaint that got her sent here. We believe her. None of us have ever heard of a neighbor being able to have another neighbor involuntarily committed. That's so terrible."

"If only we could do something about this, but we can't," another nurse added, voicing her support. "We have to treat her like any other patient."

It seemed a good sign to know that the nurses believed in Carol and supported her.

Later I had the opportunity to read a nurse's report on Carol for that day. The notes boded well for Carol's hearing. As the nurse wrote: Pt. has presented pleasant and cooperative this a.m. still with stress over pending court and mental health evaluation. Compliant with medication... Pt. progressing toward goal — has complied with any request made today.

Carol continued to feel a little better, spending time reading in her room, exchanging pleasantries with a few other patients and staff, and speaking calmly in her group therapy sessions. She took the pills the nurses offered her quietly and without struggle. *Cooperate,* she kept telling herself, *and things will go easier for you.*

To Carol, there seemed little she could do about anything in this place. For most of her adult life, she had felt she had at least some say over matters affecting her. But now, she had no say whatsoever. And if she fought back, the nurses would simply note this behavior in their black report book. Carol worried that a bad report might allow a judge to consign her to even more time on the ward.

So you had just better get control of yourself, Carol reasoned. *There's not much else you can control while in this place, but at least you can control you.*

But as the hearing began getting closer, everything started weighing heavily on Carol's mind: *What would happen if things do not go well; if the judge believes the lies told about me and doesn't hear or listen to my side of the story? What if I am sentenced to spend weeks, if not years, cooped up in a place like this? Or worse, what if I end up being sent to jail after the court case?*

Thoughts like this filled Carol with a deep sadness: *How could what is happening to me happen in the country I so strongly embraced when I first came here as a student? I've been thrown into this hospital with no chance to appeal, and simply on the urgings of a neighbor! It reminds me of how the Nazis used this tactic to put people in prisons if they seemed like an enemy of the state. I never thought such a thing could ever happen in the U.S.! Back when I took the oath for citizenship, I fervently believed the U.S. stood for freedom and civil liberties. I guess I was naïve.*

But now, it seems, the "treatment" I've suffered could happen to anyone under seemingly normal circumstances. The very real threat that anyone, at any time, and under any circumstances, could suddenly be locked up without due process is scary. Normally "due process" means you have a right to confront your attacker, and you were supposed to be presumed innocent before being found guilty. But the police never read me my rights, never questioned me, and never took my statement. And then my lawyer erroneously advised both me and Paul not to testify — so here I am, thrust into this alien system and place. If this could happen to me, it could happen to anyone! A few people or a group of them — your co-workers; friends; family; whomever — could hate you for whatever reason — like they did me — then attack you with lies, and you might not be able to protect yourself adequately from the attack.

When she felt desperate or vulnerable, Carol chose to speak to one of the nurses on duty describing her fears.

"Don't worry," the nurses urged. "The staff here isn't working against you. We're here to help, and you'll be able to defend yourself at the hearing." (They were referring to a possible hearing at which Carol's involuntary commitment could be extended.)

Tests Loom

On Monday, a psychologist, Dr. Ingram, came by to interview Carol as background for all the tests she was supposed to take the next morning.

In the interview, Dr. Ingram asked Carol about her work, home, and neighborhood. She answered fully and completely, though she sometimes shook a little with anxiety, and sometimes tears came to her eyes, as she thought about how much she missed her children, her home, her pets, and me. She didn't even have much privacy the few times she spoke to her children when they called.

Dr. Ingram took notes as she spoke, noting that her, "...speech is clear and appropriate. At times, tearful."

Then, he asked, "Any thoughts or feelings about suicide or homicide?"

"No, no," Carol said, and it was true.

"Very good," Dr. Ingram said. "What about any auditory or visual hallucinations?"

"No, no, none of that," Carol responded. "I see and hear what's going on around me. I know what's real, and I can tell when I'm just thinking or imagining something."

Dr. Ingram then handed Carol a list of adjectives, and a scale with the numbers from one to five on it, with one being best and five being worst.

"Please rate your feelings," Dr. Ingram explained.

Carol went down the list, which had words like "friendly," "happy," "angry" on it. Mostly she checked off the number "three" for each one, since she was operating mostly in neutral now. She had been trying to keep her emotions flat, to protect herself from the pain of feeling anything.

But when Carol she got to the word "depression," she gave it a "four." There was no denying it: She felt pretty lethargic and discouraged about her situation and strongly feared the upcoming test, as it could help seal her fate in a court trial.

At one time, Carol might have seen these questions as an intrusion on her privacy, but she had learned through her awful experience that the best way to exist in this system, regardless of how repressive or oppressive it seemed, was *to comply. Just follow the rules. Go along, and do everything they wanted her to do.* So that's what she did, quietly and calmly answering the questions and filling in any responses. Answering the psychologist's questions and filling in the answer form was all part of her decision to "...go along to get along" — and possibly get off the ward as soon as she could.

Finally, Dr. Ingram briefed Carol on the tests she would take the following day — one for a psychological evaluation, and another two tests to assess her cognitive skills and memory.

Later that night when I came by, Carol expressed apprehension about the upcoming tests. I found it hard to calm her down.

"I just don't know what will happen. I'm so afraid," Carol admitted. "The tests could decide everything: whether they think I'm sane; whether they think I'm mentally disturbed. And a judge will look at the results to decide whether to believe me, or believe I really did try to run over that kid." Carol was even more nervous when she added, "And I'm even more concerned about taking a memory test, because I'm afraid it might show I'm coming down with Alzheimer's. So I'm not sure I'm willing to take that test."

"Look, it'll be all right. I'm sure you'll do fine," I told Carol again and again.

But she had a hard time accepting that she really would do fine. Instead, she kept worrying about the worst-case scenario, which meant either going to jail or being confined to a mental institution for months, if not years.

"At least the interview with Dr. Ingram went well and he was very compassionate," she added.

"That's good," I said. "Just stay positive, and I'm sure everything will be fine tomorrow."

Carol nodded weakly and still apprehensive about what was to come. I left, wishing her well and urging her to relax and get a good night's sleep for the tests the next day.

Just as Carol was settling into bed that evening, Dr. Kaczmarek stopped by her room at 9:30 p.m.

Why so late again? Carol wondered.

"So how do you feel today?" Dr. Kaczmarek asked.

For a moment, Carol glared at him, upset about his timing.

"Yes, but I'm upset that you changed my medication," she said after a brief hesitation.

Dr. Kaczmarek sat down in the chair across from her bed.

"Well, I thought we would start over with your meds, so we have better control of how what you are taking is affecting you. I wanted to start you back on your meds in the morning on a lower dose."

Carol simply nodded, helpless to do anything more.

When he left, Carol lay back on the bed to go to sleep, feeling calmer and more peaceful, hopeful that tomorrow would be a better day.

But her fears began to get to her again. Though the preliminary psychological assessment had gone well, revealing no serious problems apart from the curtain of depression that surrounded her, she thought of the test as a reminder that she was being observed, analyzed, and judged every single second of her day. Plus… there was the looming specter of the court case. As an on-duty nurse walked by her room, Carol called to her, eager to talk about her confused mix of feelings.

"I feel so angry, yet fearful," Carol explained. She recounted her story about the lying kids and the social-worker neighbor falsely diagnosing her with a condition of mental illness.

"Well, you have good reason to be angry," the nurse agreed after hearing about the events. "But to heal you have to let that anger go. And it's obvious you have a deep fear underlying that anger; perhaps it's your fear of maybe going to jail about false claims of things you did which you say you didn't. Identifying the emotions and fears behind your anger will help you release those underlying feelings. Then the anger itself will go away."

Carol thanked the nurse for her insights.

Under a Microscope

In the morning, Carol experienced a battery of tests. The first one, the psychological evaluation test, had 567 questions in it! Carol answered these questions as fast as she could and to the best of her ability.

The questions ranged from the ordinary and mundane to the intrusive and prying. They queried her as to whether she had a good appetite and or liked certain magazines, and asked about bodily functions, thoughts, and common emotional responses.

As she responded, Carol tried not to think about the reasons for the odd mix of questions. But later on, she told me she believed the very ordinary questions were a foil to temper the more revealing questions. Their inclusion might make the test-taker more willing to give true answers to the intimate probing ones.

Then, it was time for an intelligence test to measure Carol's verbal and performance abilities. Carol had several hundred more questions to answer! There were questions about everyday events and items. The questions asked her, among other things, to explain what should be done in certain circumstances, the meaning of proverbs, and the reason why certain societal practices are followed. The test also included some simple arithmetic problems and word definitions, as well as identifying the missing part of a picture, arranging red and white blocks to match a design, matching symbols, and ordering pictures to tell a story.

Next, Carol took a memory test designed to measure five different types of memory — auditory, visual, working, immediate, and delayed.

It wasn't until the early afternoon that Carol was done. After the testing was over, she felt lighter, freer. Like the worst was over.

Back in the dayroom, she greeted several patients and joined a small group where she described her experience.

As Carol returned to her room, accompanied by one of the nurses whom she had gotten to know, she noticed on the other side of a glass door some members of the criminally insane ward. They were wearing orange uniforms and their heads were shaven, like prisoners in a Soviet gulag or Nazi death camp. They walked around in a daze, like zombies. *How miserable*, Carol thought. *They look like they have been heavily sedated. I've never seen such misery in my life. At least I'm not on that ward. Things could be even worse. I almost landed there.*

A little while later, Carol started feeling anxious, and went to the nurse's station to ask for a tranquilizer.

"It's because my lawyer is coming to see me about my hearing," she told the nurse. "I feel nervous about what could happen."

The nurse gave Carol a pill in a cup to swallow. "This should help," she assured Carol.

Carol and I then met with our lawyer Guildenstern.

Guildenstern told her things were "going well," and I was amazed and angered by how blasé he seemed. This was the first time we saw him since the hearing, and I felt he owed us a big apology for his bad strategy at the hearing; not telling us what to expect if things didn't go our way; and then leaving us in the lurch.

But all we heard on this subject was his opinion: "No other judge would have committed Carol."

Well, that didn't really help! It angered me that Guildenstern accepted no responsibility for the turn of events. And, since he had led us into this situation through his unfounded optimism before, I was not buying into his positive outlook this time. His examination of Odie at the commitment hearing gave me no confidence in his ability to deal with kids who might not be telling the truth on a witness stand. Frankly, I wanted to fire him, but I knew that would leave Carol feeling in the lurch, totally defenseless. So I remained calm and quiet, not wanting to upset Carol, who just sat there and took in what he said without showing any emotional reaction to his words.

Guildenstern concluded the meeting with, "I just need you to sign a release, so I have your permission to talk to Dr. Kaczmarek about how you are doing."

Carol signed. After he left, we were both hopeful that Guildenstern's meeting with Kaczmarek would go well and potentially help the outcome of her case.

The nurse on duty that night wrote in her notes: "Speech is clear and appropriate. Anxious…Remains preoccupied with court proceedings and 'the incident' that brought her here. Cooperative. Interacts with peers. States that her mood is good and rates depression at a level three."

Last Day on the Ward

Finally, there was only one day left of what had originally was supposed to be a seven-day commitment. The staff had decided to release Carol a day early, having decided that she was not mentally disturbed at all, only seriously depressed about her situation.

As you might imagine, Carol was looking forward to going home.

The morning of her release, she woke up with no complaints, and participated actively at the group discussion after breakfast. She even gave some of the other patients advice on what to do to better their own situations.

The day of Carol's early release, I arrived thinking I would be meeting with both Carol and her doctor. But when Kaczmarek arrived, he asked that Carol wait outside in the hallway while the two of us talked privately.

"What did you know about the incident with the car?" he asked me inquisitively, as if trying to make sense of the situation for himself.

"Just what Carol told me, since, from where I was standing, I couldn't see the interaction. I know that as she was driving off, she did hit the neighbor's car by accident, undoubtedly because the kids making Nazi salutes and mocking her rattled her. But a boy made up a story about her trying to run him over with her car, and then he got a friend and father to support his story. From my own personal observation I know that just like me, one of the boys, Odie Odom, would have been unable to see what he claimed to have seen at the hearing. He wasn't in a location where he could have seen what went on."

"Well, I believe your wife too," the doctor assured me. "From what she told me about herself and what happened, I don't think she could or would have done what the neighbors claim. I think what happened is terrible.

"But I find it very hard to understand what happened and why," the doctor continued. "I actually know Brody Odom, since he's a social worker and part of the mental health community in Big Pebble. It's small enough that virtually everyone in the community knows everyone else! I have no idea what could have made him resort to pushing for this crazy involuntary commitment. I don't understand what he could have against Carol to lead him to make such a charge."

"I don't either," I admitted. "It's bizarre and has been extremely stressful."

"I agree," he commiserated. "If it's any consolation, I think that Butler, or the guy who called Carol a 'Nazi' in front of kids, could be charged with a hate crime. I think his doing that is especially strange since it effectively violates the Hippocratic Oath he took as a medical doctor."

I was surprised he felt so strongly about this and encouraged by his support, but I remained concerned that the charges that had been leveled at Carol were more important to counter than to take any action against Butler.

Our conversation went on further while Carol paced in the hallway.

"I wanted to tell you all this privately, since I don't want to upset Carol any more now by reliving everything," Dr. Kaczmarek explained to me. "Tell her later, when she feels ready to discuss our conversation. I also wanted to mention that I think you both have the basis for a civil action against everyone involved in making these false charges, and I'll be glad to help if you do take any action."

Finally, our discussion over, I returned to talk to Carol.

"Do you feel ready to go home now?" I asked her.

"Yes, I want to go home now; as soon as possible!" she said with a warm smile.

"Then I'll see what I can do," I said, returning her smile.

A few minutes later, when I had officially secured her release, Carol went up to the nurses on duty to thank them for everything.

"You've been so wonderful...so helpful!" Carol gushed. "You all were there for me when I was at my lowest, and I want to thank you for all you have done."

"Well, we don't think you ever should have been committed here against your will," one of the nurses said.

"All of us always thought you were perfectly normal, and didn't display any signs of mental illness," another nurse pointed out.

"You were just very upset about things — and that's natural, given your unusual situation," offered a third.

Then, amidst their hugs and good wishes, I escorted Carol into the elevator. It was finally time to go home.

We felt a rush of freedom as we headed to the car and drove home.

In a kind of macabre epilogue, a few weeks later, we received a bill for $8,000 for Carol's stay in the ward. How ironic that we were expected to pay for her commitment, as it had been done against Carol's will!

At Guildenstern's suggestion, I referred the matter to our insurance company, who took care of the charges. And since I worked for the state that meant ultimately the taxpayers of East Kansas footed the bill.

But had we had no insurance, the gross injustice would have been that our neighbor managed to get Carol committed to a hospital against her will for a mental evaluation—and we would have been forced to pay for it.

CHAPTER 5: FACING THE CHARGES

Once Carol got home in late November from the psych ward, we enjoyed a relatively peaceful time. Looming in the background was the upcoming arraignment on aggravated assault. But for a time, we tried to put any thought of what might come aside, since we were just glad the ordeal of the involuntary commitment was over.

But there were more hurdles to overcome. I made some appointments to complain to Butler and Odom's UEKMS supervisors, and I brought the matter to the Office of Faculty Affairs. In all cases, I was told there was nothing that UEKMS could do concerning the off-campus behavior of their employees, however regrettable that behavior had been.

With Guildenstern's blessing, I contacted the National Conference for Community and Justice, as it was known for mediating serious disputes. They told me there was nothing they could do since a criminal trial was pending.

Then, we had a brief criminal court hearing on November 25 at which Carol pled "not guilty." Guildenstern sought the assurances of the judge that a "no contact" order previously issued by the court would still allow Carol to come and go from our house, and he received them. Also, the judge scheduled a further hearing for an update on the case on January 9.

In the meantime, Guildenstern advised us not to have any contact with our neighbors.

"Anything you do or say could be used against you in the upcoming criminal proceeding," he told us. "You don't want to give them any more ammunition that they might use against you."

"Okay," I agreed, deferring to his supposed expertise. "But not just one, but two, kids are lying, and that must be why the whole neighborhood seems out to get us. What about if we put up a sign in our front yard that said something like, 'Tell your mom the truth;' 'What if your child is lying?' or 'Can you be sure your child is telling you the truth?'"

Guildenstern looked aghast, so I patiently explained. "You've just told us we can't talk to our neighbors, so how else are they going to find out the truth about what went on? This might be a good idea, especially as there have been previous incidents where Tina White assumed her son Willie was telling the truth, and he wasn't."

With a slow shake of his head, Guildenstern dismissed my idea. "It's not a good idea. Your neighbors would see it as a provocation, and it could be used at the trial against Carol. I must dissuade you from doing anything of the sort."

I backed down.

Keeping an Eye Out

Carol and I still wanted to observe what was going on in the neighborhood, so I continued to use the video camera I had previously set up in our front window to record what the kids were up to without having to stare out the windows ourselves. Since our neighbors already had interpreted this as a hostile act, it didn't seem like it would make much difference for us to continue to use this already-set-up camera.

It soon became clear that just as they had before the October 23 car incident, the kids still acted as if they owned the intersection and neighborhood. Often traffic had to come to a stop because of their antics, or make a detour around them. Nor did they seem scared or even pay much attention to either of us when Carol or I drove our car in or out of our driveway in the intersection.

The children continued to act in a way that was inconsistent with the charges that had been brought against Carol. They showed no worry or concern that Carol was going to assault them with either her car, or her person.

Such behavior appeared to contradict Willie's aggravated assault claim.

A Conundrum!

Since our lawyer had advised us not to speak with our neighbors, Carol and I had no way to know if the parents learned, or came to believe, their kids were lying. For the two us, though, it was hard for us to imagine that the parents didn't know the truth. Maybe they suspected it was a made-up story, were in denial, or simply didn't care to know. But here too, *if the parents didn't know the kids were lying, it was surprising that they let their kids continue to play in the street right next to our house. After all, if the kids were to be believed, Carol was capable of acting like a homicidal maniac! So their unsupervised kids might be in real danger of a future attack if they didn't stop their play in front of our house.*

On the other hand: *Any sane and moral parent who realized their kid was lying and that this might come out in court would have immediately pulled the plug on the aggravated assault charge. Why would they support a bogus charge against Carol, to the potential peril of their own child?*

Either way, it bothered us.

The whole situation just didn't make sense.

Worries and Concerns

The charge against Carol had already caused us so much grief, and as the days passed, worries continued to weigh on us. One day I called Guildenstern to ask him what we might do to help us get through it all.

"Can we institute any legal action against the Odoms?" I asked. "After all, they started this with their false claims, and it's been a nightmare for us."

Guildenstern advised us, "No. *Don't do anything.* It is best to wait until after the criminal trial before you institute any legal action. This way, it doesn't look like you are trying to dissuade him from pursuing the criminal action."

I agreed to wait.

Around the Thanksgiving holiday, numerous concerns continued to bother Carol and me. One was the threat that Carol could spend many years in jail. Our lawyer considered that outcome unlikely — but now we had no faith in his ability to predict the outcome when it came to Carol! As you know, he had also thought the judge would throw out the mental illness claims at the involuntary commitment hearing, and that's why he hadn't prepared any evidence to refute the claim. Because of this misjudgment, Carol ended up spending over five days locked up on a psych ward against her will.

Another concern was that the teenagers who had lied at the police station and/or at the hearing seemingly had experienced no repercussions for their untruths. They hadn't even been challenged over what they said!

Next, even if Carol was ultimately found innocent at the aggravated assault trial, waiting for the outcome of the trial meant living for several months amongst our hostile neighbors. The "no contact" order when it came to our neighbors was especially bothersome and worrisome: *How could we not have any contact with any neighbors if we lived on the same street with them?*

We also experienced uneasiness about whether Guildenstern had sufficient experience in dealing with teenagers who didn't tell the truth to properly represent us at the trial. *Should we find another attorney to represent us? But if so, then he'd have to come fully up to speed on our case. Were we up for that? If we kept our lawyer, could Guildenstern be successful in negotiating reduced charges for Carol?*

And we kept thinking again and again about how to best present our case: *For example, did it make any sense to call on some of the kids who continued to play on the street as witnesses at the trial? Didn't their continued nonchalant play right in front of our home indicate that they didn't consider Carol any kind of threat?*

One day, I chose to pour out my feelings of frustration in an email to Guildenstern. In part, I wrote:

…Facing the prospect of Carol spending the better half of her remaining life in the penitentiary makes me extremely uneasy.

…The "no contact" clauses force us to avoid the neighbor(s). Living this way for months is going to be sheer misery, [as] we have to endure an intolerable situation for what is likely to be several months. Even at the end of that time, if we achieve vindication, we will still have to deal with neighbors that have harmed us deliberately and who would be extremely unlikely to apologize.

…In addition, it bothers me that adolescents seem to be granted more penalty-free lenience than adults with respect to fibs they can tell and charges they can make.

…The fact that kids in the neighborhood are still playing unabated and often unsupervised in the intersection since October 23 indicates to us that they don't seriously consider Carol to be a menace. It seems to me that they are likely to have heard the truth from Willie White and Odie Odom. Would it make sense to determine the names of some of these kids so that they could be called as witnesses at the criminal trial?

It also continued to frustrate Carol and me that Odom had used his influence as a social worker to initiate the commitment proceedings against Carol. So even if it might not be wise to file a lawsuit against Odom, what about filing a complaint about him with the East Kansas Social Worker Licensing Board? I knew that Odom's license was up for renewal in the next week, so the timing would be good. So I also asked Guildenstern about this potential course of action in an email.

Guildenstern wrote back a few minutes later to say he was in trial this week, so he wasn't available to discuss the situation.

I wrote back immediately, asking that he just tell me a "YES (go ahead) or NO (don't do it) answer" about whether to file the complaint with the Social Worker board. "I don't even have to have your reason for saying 'yes' or 'no,'" I added.

He responded with only one word: "WAIT." And so that's what I did.

Taking Its Toll — on Both of Us!

The events and concerns were taking a toll, not just on Carol, but also on me. The previous month, I also had just finished an exhausting grant application, and my father had passed away. And I still had to contend with all the events and negativity in my wife's case!

For the first time ever in my life, I arranged to meet a psychiatrist. I chose someone who also worked at UEKMS to discuss how the case was affecting me.

At our first session, I told her, "I feel things are spinning very much out of control."

After I described my current situation, the psychiatrist asked a lot of questions about my growing up as a kid. I saw her four times, but got no useful suggestions from her! At one point, she even suggested that Carol and I try ballroom dancing.

At our session the day before the upcoming arraignment, the psychiatrist said, "Yes, your situation is catastrophic and cataclysmic. But I don't have any magic wand to wave to fix things."

I determined this would be our last session. Nothing she had said to me proved worthwhile or even constructive.

Nothing Was Going Our Way

My anger and frustration continued to grow, since while Carol and I were suffering so from this case, the neighborhood kids seemed to take what was happening as a big joke. For example, on December 7, I left to go on a short errand. Willie White (the boy who had claimed Carol tried to run him over), and Tim Cutter (the son of a family that lived around the corner) were playing basketball in front of the Odom's house. When I returned from my errand, Tim Cutter screamed in mock horror at the sight of my car and ran off into the Odom's front yard. At the same time, Willie White lay down on the street, as if I had hit him with my car.

Obviously, the kids considered our situation a big, fat joke.

However, with the holidays coming up, Carol and I decided to put any thoughts of the case, and the neighbors and their kids, away. We wanted to try and enjoy the holidays as best we could.

Even this mutual decision went awry, though.

Shortly before Christmas, we got a notice that Judge Bobby Self had been assigned to the case. Guildenstern explained to Carol and me that now, "…there must be a jury trial, because I cannot let you opt to have your case heard and decided by this judge alone."

"Why not?" I asked. *Wouldn't it be faster and less expensive to have an impartial judge deal with the matter?*

"Because," Guildenstern explained, "Self is known as 'a prosecutor's judge.' That means he is likely to come down hard on Carol. I would feel very uncomfortable letting him rule on the case rather than a jury."

Great. More bad news.

"Can we request another judge?" I questioned.

"No. You have to have a good reason for this, such as a clear conflict of interest or bias, and we don't have that. Just know it's better not to go before this judge without a jury."

The thought of having to present our side of the case to a jury seemed daunting, But Guildenstern didn't trust this particular judge not to have a bias, and the last thing we wanted was for Carol to have to live the rest of her life in prison. So despite the potential expense and stress, we agreed with him.

Knowing that there was to be a jury trial, I asked Guildenstern, "What about the witnesses we will need? Can you interview the kids who would be potential witnesses?"

The suggestion made Guildenstern uncomfortable. "The kids need to be handled with kid gloves because they are juveniles. Oh, and we would need to ask their parents' permission."

"Then, can you get that, and then do the interviews?" I pressed.

"Well, that'll be complicated, and it'll take time," he hedged.

"So why not start the process now?" I suggested. "The trial is still several months away, so we have the time, right?"

Guildenstern claimed he was "too busy" with other cases. I had the feeling he just didn't want to try to interview the kids.

The prosecutor's office faxed Guildenstern the police report on December 22, and our lawyer shared it with us a day or two before Christmas. At the same time, he assured us this wasn't a case that the prosecutor, Jim Root, was likely to pursue with much vigor.

What reason did he have for thinking this way?

Guildenstern explained. "I think Root has reservations about trying this case, because his wife, who is a psychiatrist, has major reservations about it."

"What kind of reservations?" I probed.

"Just that she has worked with kids, and doesn't believe all the things she has been reading or hearing about Carol being as crazy as she's reported to be."

We were relieved to hear this. We didn't consider the possibility that Root might be leading Guildenstern to be overconfident.

But Carol and I had more misgivings about Guildenstern's current handling of our case when we read through the police file. Although by law, the prosecution is supposed to provide the defense with all of the evidence they have against a defendant, it was apparent that some key evidence was missing. Most significantly, there was no statement from Odie Odom — something we knew existed when he went to the police station to testify against Carol for the involuntary commitment hearing. So why he wasn't he being included as a witness?

I pointed out the omission to Guildenstern, explaining that the police report mentioned Odie as a witness, and that a summary of the report even pointed out his involvement, stating that: William White told Officers he was on his skateboard and Ms. Clark-Brakke attempted to run him over... she struck a parked 2001 Nissan [Xterra] and then drove off. A witness, Odie Odom, date of birth March 29, 1996, also witnessed this incident and gave the same statement to police.

So why wasn't Odie's statement transcribed and a part of the report? Had he been interrogated separately, as he should have been? If it was inadvertently missing (or intentionally), what else might be missing from the evidence the prosecutor had about the case? Did he not have it, or was he deliberately keeping it from us?

Carol and I began to become paranoid over what was missing or being withheld from us — but Guildenstern was dismissive of such concerns.

"Don't worry," he told me. "Prosecutors frequently leave out evidence they should send to defense attorneys. It happens all the time. So you just have to request what you think is missing and they'll give it to you."

What you *"think"* is missing? *How would you even know what was missing if you didn't already know about it?* Carol and I only knew what we did because of the evidence used against Carol in the involuntary commitment hearing. *Was there anything else singled out by the prosecutor and "reserved" for the aggravated assault hearing?*

Guildenstern didn't seem especially concerned, and when I asked him to request the missing documents from the prosecutor, he begged off doing anything immediately. He reiterated he was very busy, and therefore unable to do anything until after the New Year.

Carol and I went to the prosecutor's office ourselves to obtain a copy, only to be told by the clerk at the front desk said the office could not give one to us.

"That's only released to your attorney as part of discovery under a subpoena. But if you're involved in the case, you can get a copy from the police department."

And so that's what we decided to do.

What Were We Thinking?

At this point, dear reader, you might feel Carol and I were, well crazy to continue with Guildenstern. We frequently didn't see eye-to-eye with the man; and he sometimes failed to recognize, address, or seemingly even care about our concerns, legitimate or not. Worse, he had let us down badly in the commitment hearing!

The truth of the matter is that *I had wanted to jettison him for quite some time.* But he wasn't representing me; he was representing Carol, and Carol wasn't ready to abandon the only person she knew who might be capable of protecting her. It was her decision and hers alone. She and I discussed changing lawyers several times, but Carol consistently indicated she wasn't ready for a change. He had been with us from the beginning, and she wanted him to continue on her case.

Meanwhile, thinking about what evidence we would need to sway a jury, I began taking pictures with our car positioned at the location where Willie claimed the incident occurred. I wanted to show that none of the kids could have really witnessed what Odie Odom had claimed at the involuntary commitment hearing, *because they weren't in a physical location that allowed them to see the event.*

Was Divorce an Instigator?

Just after Christmas, Carol discovered some information that led us to believe there might be some ulterior motive for the parents and kids who were supporting Willie's version of events. She learned that before the car incident, Willie White had refused to have anything to do with his father. But through supporting his son's lie, William had seized upon an opportunity to act as the great protector and champion of his son, and their father-son relationship began to improve.

Then, Carol and I noticed a "For Sale" sign in front of the Cutter's home the day after Christmas. When we heard that the Cutters had recently divorced, the two of us began to speculate amongst ourselves that, like Willie, their son Tim might have experienced similar issues from being in a fractured family, making him extra-willing to be a strong supporter of Willie's — no matter what the concocted tale.

Carol and I believed Guildenstern might be able to use the close relationship between some of the boys to procure evidence to help discredit them in the case against Carol. As Carol wrote to Guildenstern the next morning: I think the Cutters' boy Timothy is important to me, because he confided that Willie needed a lot of attention... Why [has] nobody has ever attempted to interview any of the neighbors since most of them know Willie?

Success! Guildenstern finally agreed to follow one of our leads! He told us he had arranged to talk with Tim through his mother.

Little did we realize that Guildenstern did not plan to conduct that interview for several months.

Bombshells

I did the best I could to stay hopeful and keep Carol's spirits up for the arraignment the next morning on January 9, 2009, at the Circuit Court of Podleski County in East Kansas. Judge Bobby Self would preside, and this would be the first time Carol and I would see the man and get a sense of him in person. Carol had previously pled "not guilty" at the initial arraignment; this was to be a more formal arraignment dealing with the pleadings and preliminary motions in the case.

"I'm very scared," Carol told me, and I replied, "Don't be. Remember that Guildenstern seems to think Root, the prosecutor, is sympathetic."

The morning of the arraignment arrived. I nervously drove Carol to the courthouse, an old ornate building located in downtown Big Pebble. Guildenstern was sitting on a bench outside the courtroom waiting for us.

As we approached, he laid a bombshell on us. He told us he had received a call from Deputy Prosecutor Jim Root the afternoon before.

"There'll be two motions today," he said, "although I'm not too concerned about either of them, just annoyed that Root only told me about them at five p.m. yesterday. The first is a 'stay-away' motion designed to extend the no-contact order to include kids under sixteen for a greater distance—a mile from your house."

"And you didn't call to inform us yesterday?" I challenged heatedly, the hair on the back of my neck standing up.

Perhaps Guildenstern didn't tell us about his conversation with Root the day before because he didn't want to upset us any further on the night before the arraignment. Or maybe he didn't want to have to deal with a discussion with us last night about what to do. But whatever his reasoning was, it was a breach of trust that he didn't tell us. Anger and feelings of panic over his failure to forewarn my wife and me welled up inside of me. Receiving such news so late in the process felt like an ambush.

"There's no practical way that Carol could come and go from our house under such an order!" I shot out, horrified.

"Look, I'm sure I can reduce the distance they're calling for," Guildenstern said in a placating tone. "I wouldn't worry too much about this. The other motion is for a second mental evaluation."

I could only sputter, "But… but… but Carol was just evaluated at the Lutheran Hospital, and she got a clean bill of health. The staff there all agreed that she's fine!"

Guildenstern tried to reassure both Carol and me. "I'm sure I can successfully argue against the mental health motion. It's a motion that's frequently made by defense attorneys who plan to use an insanity defense, and we're not going to be doing so. Besides, prosecutors hardly ever request such a thing, so I don't think it'll be granted."

Whether Guildenstern planned to argue insanity or not, both Carol and I were incensed upon hearing about this planned motion. Once again, the State was portraying Carol as a lunatic. It was both unfair and unrealistic.

We became even more upset when Guildenstern mentioned a third thing that Root had told him.

In a casual tone, our lawyer informed us, "The prosecutor kind of suggested he might drop all the charges against Carol if you two moved."

"What?!" I exclaimed. We had spent time and effort to beautify our home and make it ours, and that's what it felt like to us now: *home.* Leaving might be stressful for Carol, and she was already under enough stress as it was. "Over my dead body!" I sputtered. "It's like he's blackmailing us, because the neighbors want us out."

"Yes, I understand," Guildenstern soothed. "It's just an offer. You don't need to accept it."

"Well, we certainly won't," I bit out. "But is it even legal for a prosecutor to offer or threaten such a thing?" I wondered aloud.

"It's not really normal to make such an offer during the plea-bargaining process. But Root stated this idea in such a vague hypothetical way to me that he could always have 'plausible deniability,' meaning that he could always deny he had said anything of the sort."

There was no more time to discuss the situation. It was 9 a.m.—time to go into the courtroom.

As we walked in from the side entrance open to the public, I saw the judge seated ahead of us on a raised platform. One half-dozen staff members were at a desk close to the judge; they were responsible for managing the cases on the dockets for the day. A stenographer at a computer terminal was there to record the proceedings, and a bailiff in a security officer uniform was policing the courtroom.

Just below the staffers were two lecterns where the lawyers and defendants had to stand and address the court. To the right of these were three rows of pew-style benches, which a jury would sit in if a jury trial was going on. For the moment, the benches were being used to seat prisoners dressed in orange or white jump suits and manacled together as they waited for their hearings.

On the other side of the lecterns were some seats for the lawyers and at the rear of the room were half-dozen rows of long pew-style benches that made up the gallery for the defendants waiting to be called, plus any observers.

At Guildenstern's direction, Carol and I took a seat in the front of the gallery, where we would we wait until her case was called. At that time, she would go up to one of the lecterns with Guildenstern.

Finally, after about an hour, it was time. Carol walked up to the lectern beside Guildenstern.

The judge asked, "How do you plead to the aggravated assault and first-degree criminal mischief charges?" Carol replied, "Not guilty."

At once, Root attacked.

"I know my requests for these motions are unusual," he told the judge. "But they're appropriate in a case against a woman known in her neighborhood as 'the scary old lady,' who has stood in her yard and yelled at children."

While Carol visibly cringed at this characterization of her, I thought, *that 'scary old lady' is a made-up epithet to whitewash and disguise what the kids were really calling her!*

But there was nothing for Carol or me to do but remain quiet as Root continued with his arguments to support his motions to the judge.

"This is also a case where the parents are trying to keep their children away from her. So since Clark-Brakke is free on a $5,000 bond, she should be barred from having any contact with children under age sixteen within a one-mile radius of her home. I know that no-contact orders are usually limited to individuals, not whole groups of people. But I have sought this order because the neighborhood children have to walk by her home to get to school. And the order would only apply to these neighborhood children. It wouldn't prevent Clark-Brakke from being around the children of relatives and friends."

Guildenstern raised objections.

"This order is totally unnecessary. The one-mile area is too wide. This order will interfere with her going into her own home. What is she supposed to do? We'd like to modify the order to only bar her from *initiating* contact with children."

Root shot back, "The order only prevents her from contacting the children directly. Besides, Clark-Brakke should know how to conduct herself. She's old enough to know not to yell at children. She knows to go to the parents. [*Not according to the no contact order already in place.*] She can go to the police. Besides, she has no basis for yelling at the kids anyway. I live in the neighborhood, and I've gone jogging through this intersection. I never saw any problem caused by the kids to justify her behavior."

Judge Self asked both attorneys to be silent while he considered the motion.

Finally, the judge spoke. "All right. I'm going to scale back the distance to a three-block radius from the house."

This judgment spelled a small victory for us, although the no-contact order was still in place. This meant we must be especially careful until the trial: If Carol had any direct contact with anyone under age sixteen within three blocks of our house (other than for her relatives or personal acquaintances), she might face immediate arrest and detention — which could mean going to jail, or back to Lutheran Hospital.

The judge turned to the prosecutor's motion for another psychiatric evaluation by state doctors.

"Not necessary!" Guildenstern argued. "My client has no intention of offering an insanity defense. Also, the examination would mean a trial date can't be set until the examination is complete, which would take at least three months."

Worse, in his rebuttal, Root didn't refer to the results of Carol's psychiatric evaluation, saying instead, "I felt the need for this evaluation — even though prosecutors rarely request one — because of the nature of the allegations against Mrs. Clark-Brakke, the circumstances of her arrest, and *the fact that she was briefly committed to a mental hospital in November* [emphasis mine]. Moreover, she was arrested at a bar, and at the police station she was yelling and screaming."

His arguments couldn't have been more embarrassing or distorted. He mentioned that Carol was committed involuntarily — but then deliberately failed to say she had been cleared! But again, Carol and I were powerless to say anything in court ourselves; we had to rely on our lawyer to defend us. But Guildenstern seemed to be M.I.A. when it came to offering the judge a complete and accurate picture of Carol's situation.

Root kept on, giving more and more reasons as to why the evaluation was needed. He even held up the court files from Carol's mental health hearing in November!

"Your Honor," he said, "as these court files show, Clark-Brakke was committed to a mental hospital after her neighbor, Brody Odom, filed a petition in which he referred to the criminal allegations against her. And in this petition, Odom reported that Clark-Brakke curses children, and I quote, '…by getting in their face so much to where a person literally has to stand back.' Also, Odom wrote in this petition that Clarke-Brakke is… 'paranoid and makes false accusations.' And then in describing Clark-Brakke's encounter with the police, Odom wrote that he heard her accusing a police officer of being a member of the Ku Klux Klan and threatening to call Barack Obama. So, as you can see, this mental evaluation is much needed."

I shook my head in disgust. The prosecutor was using Guildenstern's failure to represent Carol properly at the involuntary commitment hearing against Carol now, with the prosecutor using those events to portray Carol as being crazy! Although Guildenstern tried to argue that Carol was not judged to be insane or a threat to anyone after her evaluation in November, Root continued to insist that the new assessment was necessary since this was now January, and Carol had a history of threatening and scaring the kids.

As a result, the judge went along with Root's request, deciding that Carol had to undergo another mental evaluation to determine her competency to stand trial. He said he could not set our trial date until he received the results of the evaluation.

When we discovered that the evaluation wouldn't be until March, it was devastating. All Carol and I wanted was for this trial to be over, and her name and reputation to be cleared! We left the courthouse shaken and very demoralized.

Guildenstern then prepared a motion for discovery in order to get the prosecutor to speedily provide a series of documents to show what evidence he had against Carol in bringing the case against her, including any exculpatory evidence the state had collected showing that Carol wasn't guilty. It was designed to force the prosecutor to show what actual evidence he had that Carol had actually committed the charged offense or that the victim or any relatives suffered any harm because of what allegedly happened.

(Author's note: In retrospect, Guildenstern's motion did little good. The prosecutor continued to withhold evidence without Guildenstern being able to compel its production. Odie Odom's statement to the police was never shown to us, although Odie was supposed to be a key witness supporting Willie's story. In fact, despite Guildenstern's motion, the prosecutor never turned over any further evidence beyond the initial faxes provided on December 22.)

Both Carol and I left the hearing that day disturbed by what had gone on, but for different reasons. She was sad and frustrated by how the prosecutor had inaccurately portrayed her, then twisted the particulars of her case. She also was stupefied about having to undergo another mental health evaluation, and distraught at the thought that she would have to wait months for her trial to start. Carol wanted it all to be over!

As for me, my thoughts raged over how the lawyer had handled our case. Guildenstern had led us like lambs to the slaughter yet again. He should have informed us the day before upon hearing of the motions, and he should have countered today's request for a new mental evaluation much more forcefully. He seemed to be no better at defending us against a prosecutor and judge than he had been at the involuntary commitment hearing!

Once again, he had set us up, let us down, and played into the hands of the prosecutors. As far as I was concerned, I wanted to fire him, but Carol still had confidence in him and over the next few days, she continued to insist we retain him.

For me though, it was strike two against Guildenstern.

The Nightmare Continues; the Mystery Deepens

The following day, I picked up the local paper in front of our house, and our nightmare got worse. On the first page of the local news section of the *East Kansas Republic-Tribune* was an article about the hearing that announced, "Woman ordered to take mental exam, avoid kids." Then it proceeded to outline the case from the prosecutor's point of view, noting how Carol was known in her neighborhood as the "scary old lady" who stood in her yard, yelled at children, and allegedly tried to run down a twelve-year old boy.

Seeing the article was devastating. As we read through it, we were aghast at the way Carol was presented as a crazy old lady; it was as if she was the local witch of the neighborhood! It was all from the point of view of the prosecutor, and no doubt did plenty to convict Carol in the court of public opinion.

I called Guildenstern to complain.

"Can't we get a retraction or another article from Carol's point of view?"

Guildenstern said we couldn't do anything; the press was free to print what it wanted, and it could present any point of view, as long as the facts were correct, which they were, although clearly slanted to make Carol appear crazy.

"Well, it is unfortunate, but there's really nothing to do about it," Guildenstern added. "The reporter Jim Larson is a good guy, and a good court reporter. That's just the breaks."

After I hung up, I was so angry at Guildenstern's unconcerned attitude that I started to look into other attorneys to replace Guildenstern that very day, although I realized that I would have to wait until Carol was fed up with him first. And for now, she seemed to be in denial that he had done such a bad job representing her. She was so depressed by the outcome of the hearing and no-contact order, the prospect of still another mental evaluation, and the damning article about her, that she wasn't ready to seriously consider dismissing Guildenstern yet.

Instead, on the following day, Carol sent Guildenstern a follow-up letter about the hearing. She was especially concerned with setting the record straight to counter all the lies and false allegations against her. As she wrote, why wasn't my mental health record from Lutheran that could have been presented at that hearing not available? I will pick up that record tomorrow from Lutheran and bring it to the prosecutor's office, if you would be so kind to give me his name and current address... I would like to set the record straight... Second... in the police report part of the Odom boy's testimony was missing. I would like to pick it up tomorrow. Where can I go to do so? I want to pick up the transcript of the very first hearing. Where can I get it? When will the truth finally be revealed? Do I have to live with all these lies and all the allegations the rest of my life?

Guildenstern wrote back telling Carol that a file "...often gets piecemealed as various reports are described," and not to go to any of these places to get her report herself. His response was in screaming CAPS: "LET ME EMPHASIZE THAT IT WILL BE COUNTERPRODUCTIVE FOR YOU TO GO PERSONALLY TO THESE PLACES. I WILL TAKE CARE OF IT."

On reading his letter, Carol became livid. *Why shouldn't she be able to pick up her own mental health file? Why shouldn't she be able to refute all the lies told about her? And why shouldn't she get the complete police report? Wasn't a defendant supposed to be innocent until proven guilty?*

Carol responded with another email:

You say 'counterproductive.' I have the right to pick up my mental health file and deliver it to the prosecutor. What is his name and address?

I want to counter all the lies that have been in circulation since October. Nobody, I tell you, nobody, could live with such a burden for any length of time.

I want the complete police report. If they do this in bits and pieces, they need to be told that this is inefficient and counterproductive for people who are accused of a crime. Nobody who is a professional can deliver a report in bits and pieces...Whatever happened to the notion, INNOCENT UNTIL PROVEN GUILTY?"

Guildenstern immediately wrote back:

"It is a BAD IDEA to do that. That is why you have a lawyer."

Now Carol was beginning to doubt Guildenstern too. Together the two of us went to the police department to get an official signed copy of the complete police file, which they gave to us without objection. Although there were interviews in it with Willie White and Johnny Boyle, there was only a case report in which one of the officers stated that Odie Odom told him that he "...witnessed Clark-Brakke attempt to run over White with her vehicle." *There was no statement or transcript from Odie Odom in the file.*

Why not? Was evidence was being withheld from our lawyer and us? At the involuntary commitment hearing on November 14, 2008, the father-and-son team clearly indicated that they gave a statement to the police at the police station on the evening of October 23, 2008. The police case file even stated on the last page that, "...Mr. White and his mother came to the Detective Division along with the witness Odie Odom and his father to give statements."

Why leave this out? Could it be that Odie and his father didn't want the boy's statement used any longer, because both knew it was a lie? Or was it the police that had little confidence in Odie's statement?

We asked to speak to the lead police lieutenant, but when we did, he simply assured us: "Everything's there."

The answer didn't satisfy. We weren't content with that, since the lieutenant might not really know, and might just be giving us a canned "everything's fine" answer without bothering to check. Or, maybe he really did know, but was withholding the statement at the prosecutor's request... Thus, we asked to speak with the officer who supposedly took the statements from the witnesses that day in October. She told us there was no statement from Odie Odom, even though the police case file stated there was. We left the police station feeling like we were in some kind of Kafka-like mystery, where nothing is as it is claimed to be, and one faces a bureaucratic tangle of denial and lies. Everything seemed bizarre and crazy, and we felt hopeless and abandoned.

Guildenstern, through both actions and words, had made it clear he wasn't really going to help us.

Carol and I were on our own, facing a criminal justice system monster that was sucking us in and going to destroy us if we weren't able to do something to stop the process.

Another Instance of Personal Intimidation

On January 22, I took Carol to see her counselor, social worker Nelly Harper, at the UEKMS Psychiatric Research Institute. While we were sitting in the waiting room, Brody Odom, who also worked there as a social worker, came down the hall. He spotted us, then came within three feet of us to stop and talk to another patient in the room with us who was not even his patient. It was as if he wanted to show us that we were in his territory or house, and therefore subject to his power.

Carol and I sat there, intimidated. We did not want to say anything or move; we didn't want to turn this into any sort of a personal encounter with him. Fortunately, Nelly Harper came out of her office to get Carol, and saw what was going on.

After Carol got to her office, she discussed what had happened with Ms. Harper.

"Yes, I saw what occurred," Ms. Harper said. "It was wrong for Mr. Odom to do that," she concurred.

"Can we arrange for any future meetings between us to not take place on the second floor where Brody Odom might again intrude on my space in such an intimidating fashion?" Carol begged.

"Yes, that's fine," Ms. Harper readily agreed.

Trying to Set the Record Straight

Seeing how emotionally wrenching this case had been for Carol, I wanted to turn the tide. I remembered reading an article in the *East Kansas Republic-Tribune* entitled, "Pants on Fire: Truth be told, all kids tell some lies." It described how kids generally can lie, and how parents can make it safe for kids to admit their lies and tell the truth. *Reading this article might be the only way to get the Whites or Odoms to consider the possibility that their sons might be lying about Carol trying to run Willie over!*

As a result, I made a fateful decision without consulting Carol.

I waited for a time when neither the Odoms nor the Whites would be around. An opportunity arrived: the next day: All the neighborhood kids went to school, Mrs. Odom left, and Brody Odom pulled away on his motorcycle. I headed out to the street with two copies of the article, and put one in the Odom's mailbox, and one on the windshield of the White's SUV.

I felt like it was okay to do what I did because the no-contact order didn't specify me, and at the arraignment, the prosecutor and judge had specifically approved "…complaints to parents" (about their children's actions).

Unfortunately, Odom came back on his motorcycle just then, and saw me.

He looked at me steadily, but did not anything. Of course, this was nothing new: In over a year of living next to one another, he and I had never exchanged a single word. He hadn't even come over to me once to complain about Carol's supposed behavior!

In any case, Odom presumably complained about my depositing the article on his property, because three days later Guildenstern came by our house to confront me about it.

"How could you put that article in Odom's mailbox?" he yelled at me. "Now Judge Self wants both you and Carol in court this Friday to admonish you about it."

"Carol had nothing to do with this!" I advised. "So why do both of us have to appear?"

"Because this is *Carol's* case."

"But I thought at the arraignment it was stipulated that we were allowed to complain to the parents now — or isn't that the case?"

"This isn't complaining. This is *inciting*," he shot back, glaring at me like a father chastising a naughty boy. "Besides, the old no-contact order is still in effect."

At that point in our conversation, I handed Guildenstern a video recording of the kids still playing out front in the intersection and asked him to share this so that both judge and prosecutor could observe how little the kids were concerned about continuing to play in the intersection. He agreed to do so.

That Friday, Carol and I showed up with Guildenstern for a hearing with Judge Self. Root began presenting the case against me.

"Your Honor, I realize Mr. Brakke wasn't specifically included in the no-contact order. But…" he continued, his voice rising with anger, "his actions in placing an inflammatory article in Mr. Odom's mailbox and on Ms. White's SUV were clearly in violation of its intent or spirit."

I kept waiting to have a chance to explain, but Judge Self never called on me to let me speak. And Guildenstern never said anything to the judge to try and defend me. He just remained silent after Root finished his presentation and glared at me.

Judge Self then admonished Carol and me: "I'm sick and tired of these shenanigans! If you neighbors can't control yourselves in Sunken Valley, I will throw you out of your house." Then, speaking directly to me, he continued. "Now, Mr. Brakke, the no-contact order applies to you as well from now on. If you do anything like this again, I will throw you in jail for contempt. Do you understand?"

I nodded my head, but Judge Self looked at me sternly as he said, "Just nodding isn't enough. You are in a court of law, and you need to say something to show you understand."

"Yes, Your Honor, I understand." I said quietly. I did not want to do anything further to jeopardize my wife's case in the eyes of the judge.

"Very well," he said, waving us away.

As Carol and I walked out, I felt dismay that the court had castigated me. This feeling was compounded when Guildenstern told us that neither the prosecutor nor the judge had agreed to view the video recordings I had given him of kids playing in the intersection since October 23.

Still, after the hearing with Judge Self, everything seemed to return to a kind of calm. And Guildenstern began to seem like he was interested in our case! He arranged for a private investigator to come by to take measurements around the scene of the incident. Guildenstern wanted some independent verification so to back up my contention that the kids in front of the White's house, including Odie Odom, physically could not have seen what Odie had claimed to see. Finally, Guildenstern was doing something on our behalf!

On February 19, I took Carol to the East Kansas State Hospital for her second mental evaluation. The process went quickly and smoothly. She went on an outpatient basis to the office of a clinical psychologist who interviewed her for over an hour, and she had plenty of opportunity to tell her side of the story.

In the end, the psychologist Dr. Spencer told her: "I'm very perplexed why the prosecutor's office demanded this evaluation, which is normally requested by the defense counsel when planning an insanity defense. I find you very competent to stand trial." Carol was relieved. So was I. Another obstacle was cleared.

CHAPTER 6: THE MOUSETRAP

March started well enough. Carol flew to Austin for a long weekend to visit her son Henning. On the home front, the Odoms moved the basketball hoop out of the street and into their driveway. As a result, play in the intersection decreased markedly. The kids were even less likely to dart about on their scooters and skateboards in the middle of intersection.

Carol told me that she believed the calls she had been making to the police about the kids when their play was putting them in danger were responsible. Later we learned that Root, the prosecutor in Carol's case, had advised the Odoms to move the basketball hoop, but we didn't know that at the time.

Springing the Mousetrap

On the evening of March 13, Carol took our dog for a walk. Along the way, she encountered our neighbor John Smith. He was watching some kids (the group included Tim Cutter) play basketball at the school playground close by. Carol talked to Mr. Smith for a while, and remembers distractedly calling out some comments to the effect of, "Nice shot!" — but not directing them towards any particular kid.

Willie White was sitting apart from the kids playing basketball, but Carol did not interact whatsoever with him.

But apparently, all the while, Tina White was watching, and Odie Odom — whom Carol had not even seen! — was secretly videotaping Carol by the playground.

Our neighbors had sprung a mousetrap.

Three days later, Guildenstern notified us that Carol had to appear at a new hearing to determine whether she was in violation of the no-contact court order. Guildenstern told us that Carol was charged with "making contact" with children at the playground that day, and with "making animal noises."

Guildenstern was out of town, so Carol and I asked John Smith if he would be willing to refute the allegation of animal noises. He concurred that Carol had not made animal noises during their conversation. Nor had she made any untoward comments to the children playing nearby. We asked him if he would speak to our lawyer, and he agreed.

The next day, Guildenstern conferred with Smith by phone, and then Root. Our lawyer discovered that the prosecutor had already conferred with Smith, who had provided him with enough information to charge Carol with violating the no-contact order.

Root also told Guildenstern that the animal noises mentioned had happened in an entirely separate incident, one that involved Brody Odom. Carol had no idea what Odom was talking about.

Carol became distressed at the news of another hearing, and requested that the hearing be delayed until her counselor, who was out of town, could accompany her to court. The judge denied her request.

That evening, Guildenstern conferred with us at our home. It was during this conversation that Carol admitted that she had reached the point where the very sight of Brody Odom — the man who had had her involuntarily committed—was now enough to make her involuntarily throw up. She then said that it was probably the sound of this gagging that was being construed as "animal noises."

At this point, Carol lost it, hysterically declaring that she would rather be "…thrown in jail!" than have to face Odom in court without her therapist present.

I tried to calm Carol down, but when my efforts were to no avail, and she went away sobbing. I turned to ask Guildenstern if there was an alternative to Carol going to jail if she proved unwilling to attend the hearing.

He said he thought that the judge might be willing to let her go get psychiatric help by committing herself at the mental hospital.

At this point, I had to end the conversation and attend to my distraught wife. I indicated to Guildenstern that I would not hold him responsible for Carol going to jail if she failed to show up at the hearing, but that I would terminate his services if I convinced Carol to come to the hearing, and she still was sent to jail.

After Guildenstern left our home, I somehow managed to calm Carol down some and get her to agree to go to court the next day.

Trapped!

The following day, Tina White began her court testimony nearly in tears. She talked about how terrified all her children, particularly her special-needs child Wayne, were of Carol. The lie struck Carol in the heart, since she thought Wayne was a darling, and had always treated him nicely.

Tina also testified that she had heard Carol make animal noises from across the street, and that Carol had made up a lie about Tina's dog having bitten her.

As for the latest incident, she indicated that Carol had deliberately followed Willie White to the playground, which made Willie cower in fear as Carol talked to Mr. Smith. Root brandished a DVD of the videotape taken by Brody Odom as if it were the smoking gun, but it was never shown for us to look at. (Root had shown it to both Self and Guildenstern previously.) Once again, Guildenstern proved completely ineffectual in Carol's defense.

When Brody Odom took the stand, Carol threw up involuntarily. As the court adjourned briefly to allow Carol to recover, I glanced over at Odom. He was sitting on the stand *grinning.*

After the adjournment, Odom testified that Carol had made animal noises at him and children on another occasion. Guildenstern asked him what the noises sounded like, and Odom indicated they were rather like those a cat might make.

Upon hearing this, I blanched. I frequently called one of our cats in at nighttime by making cat-like calls — a routine habit I had never thought to mention to our lawyer.

Carol then took the stand. She testified that she did not follow Willie White deliberately, that she had never seen Odie Odom at the playground, and that she never directed any words other than, "Nice shot!" towards the group of kids. She also indicated that any animal noises from her were simply her retching involuntarily in the presence of Brody Odom.

When it was over, Judge Self-ruled that Carol had violated the court order, and that she had to go directly to jail. Sobbing, Carol was handcuffed and led to jail.

I went up to Guildenstern and told him that I wished for him to arrange it with the judge that Carol could commit herself to an inpatient program at Lutheran instead of being in jail.

Then I informed Guildenstern that his services were terminated once he had arranged this for us.

Committed, Again (!)

I went to visit Carol at the jail, only to be informed that the prisoners cannot receive visitors in their first seventy-two hours there. The unexpected news stunned me, and as I sat there trying to figure out what I could do for Carol, Guildenstern called to tell me that the judge would allow me to transport Carol from jail to Lutheran so long as I did not allow her to go to our home to pack anything. I did as instructed and left Carol at Lutheran sick to my stomach over what was being done to her.

The next morning, an extremely prejudicial article appeared in the *East Kansas Republic-Tribune*. It went so far as to speculate that the prosecutor's office now saw the children's use of Nazi epithets in reference to Carol as the motive for her "attack" on Willie. Reading this sickened me: *The newspaper was taking a hate crime by the kids and turning it into a weapon to be used against the victim of the hate crime!* Moreover, since the epithets the children had used hadn't been mentioned at this hearing, I could only imagine that the prosecutor must have leaked such details to the newspaper.

Once again, I brought Carol some of her belongings at Lutheran, and began visiting her there twice daily.

Back on the Psych Ward

Carol was admitted to the hospital on March 18 with "...major depressive disorder." Her whole universe was exploding on her, and even to the day of my writing this book, it is nearly impossible for her to speak about how she felt during this time.

Most of what I do know comes from the notes and reports of the nursing staff there, and Carol's doctor.

During her stay there, Carol was breaking down in tears frequently, genuinely worried about whether she would be able to return to her home one day. She stated to one of the nurses, "How could someone do this to me, just ruin my life? It seems impossible that these people could have me first committed, and then send me to jail!" When she spoke on the phone, the staff noticed that she talked loudly and tearfully, or returned to her room after every conversation to cry uncontrollably. She kept remarking, "I am being barred from my own home!"

She was unable to sleep peacefully through the night.

During her first full day in the hospital, Carol stayed in her room with the lights out and door closed, lying in bed while rocking back and forth sobbing. She also showed signs of anxiety, pacing back and forth.

By evening, she was doing better. She attended group therapy the next day, with the social worker leading the group describing her as, "Verbose... comments on every subject and on everyone else's comments. Patient was encouraging and positive until it came to the neighbors — then she wants vengeance."

But whenever Carol returned to being on her own, her anxiety and sadness returned. To handle this, she would request medication. Often her despair about not being able to return to her home gave way to feelings of anger and vengeance. At times, she refused to attend group therapy or any attempts to work on her coping skills. To top it off, Carol became physically sick, coming down with a mild case of diverticulitis.

The staff constructed this report on Carol: ...affect flat, making eye contact, and interacting appropriately with staff. 1) Coping – ineffective. Patient continues to exhibit some anxiety ...Verbalizes feelings and concerns about current situation and [not] being able to return home at this time. 2) Violence, risk for – Patient without any aggressive behavior."

Dr. Kaczmarek wrote that he felt that if Carol was not in the "secure" environment of the hospital, she would not be safe! He noted she was, "...very despondent, helpless, hopeless... despairing about this mess which seemed to start as a simple accident... very despondent about treatment by children in neighborhood."

On one of my visits, I made Carol feel worse. I told her that we had to seriously consider the possibility of moving.

I would read later that Carol stated to the staff after hearing this news from me, "It's just not fair! I just finished decorating the last room in the house. I have a beautiful garden [at my home] that has taken me a long time to grow. We just spent a lot of money on the landscaping getting it just the way we wanted it! *It's not fair.*" Carol apparently went on to demand a tranquilizer, and when the staff said they needed to check her vitals first, she grew extremely agitated.

Carol's downward spiral continued over the next few days, even after I had arranged with the court through another lawyer for Carol to go to Austin where she could be in the care of her son.

Some staff and doctor notes said about Carol at this time: ...Tearful. Anxious. States, 'I really need to find out about leaving here today or I'm going to go crazy. I can't take it anymore. Demanding to leave. States she has arranged to fly out of town tomorrow at 1700 to stay with son. ...States doctor, judge, lawyer have all agreed to these arrangements... Not emotionally stable. Tearful. Escalates... She is very anxious, fearful of accidentally 'bumping into' a neighborhood child and accused of breaking the no-contact order. She is fearful and panicky, but seemed relieved she was given permission to leave East Kansas until the hearing or trial.

On Friday, March 27, Carol was discharged so that she could go to

Austin, Texas to live with her son until the next available court date. But Judge Self wouldn't even allow her to go home to pack. While being allowed to leave gave Carol tremendous relief — she was so glad to get off the psych ward!—it also caused an even greater amount of stress, pain and misery. After all…

She was *in exile.*

She wasn't allowed back in her home.

In all the twenty-five years of our marriage, I had never seen my wife so despondent.

CHAPTER 7: LIVING IN LIMBO (AND ON THE VERGE OF A NERVOUS BREAKDOWN)

While Carol was at Lutheran, I had replaced Guildenstern. I chose Ron Priestley as our new lawyer, partly on the stupid assumption that kids on a witness stand would be intimidated by his deep voice. On March 20, I hired him. We spent less than twenty minutes talking about the case, and he indicated to me that if I wished to adopt more of a "hardball" approach to the case than Guildenstern had, I should get a different attorney. His basic message was to trust him, for he knew what he was doing due to decades of experience.

I wasn't willing to sit back and risk letting the same things happen all over again by just letting our new lawyer call all the shots. So when I kept asking him why other things couldn't be tried in our defense of Carol, he quit abruptly, after less than two weeks on the case.

I was mortified. I suspect he felt I was a pest who wasn't giving him enough latitude to do his job his way.

On March 27, Carol departed for Austin, where her son and his girlfriend took good care of her. She felt safe in their company. She walked around a nearby lake and gathered wildflowers. Her reprieve there allowed her to regain some composure.

While Carol was away, Ron Priestley emailed me that he could no longer represent her. I told Carol when I next spoke to her on the phone, and she decided to ask Guildenstern if he would be willing to represent her again. Guildenstern agreed.

Carol returned from Austin the afternoon of April 5. I picked her up at the airport but had to bring her to the Doubletree Hotel: She was still forbidden by the court from going home. Carol felt very badly about being back in Big Pebble — yet barred from entering and residing in her own home.

That afternoon, we met with Guildenstern in the hotel lobby. He brought us a copy of the report from Dr. Spencer of East Kansas State Hospital; it affirmed Carol's mental competence to stand trial. I told him Carol and I were ready to move out of the house.

Carol then asked Guildenstern to petition the judge to allow her to return home only during school hours for the next few days, when the children were not in the neighborhood. Guildenstern said he would do so, but that Carol needed to specify a chaperone for her visits home (for unknown reasons, I was not allowed to serve that purpose).

At the hearing the next day, our request that Carol be permitted to return home during school days only was permitted, on the condition that the chaperone we had put forth—the daughter of someone in my department, whom we would pay for her time—be with Carol during these visits. Carol and I were relieved; we felt that the ability to be in her own home would allow Carol to regain some of her emotional balance.

The following morning, there was an article in the *East Kansas Republic-Tribune* on our case. To our shock, the article quoted quite of a bit of the background information from Dr. Spencer's report—information that was not even supposed to be seen by the prosecutor! Even Guildenstern was shocked, but he did nothing about it.

The following day, we met with a realtor to discuss putting our home up for sale. At the same time, we began looking for another place to stay, as we had a dog and three cats. Every possibility had to be brought by Guildenstern to Root and Self for approval. After several false starts, we decided on the Visitors Inn, which was approved.

During this time leading up to the trial, Carol started to show true ill effects of her situation. She kept changing her mind about nearly every decision that had to be made about her situation. She had a period of extreme anxiety or despair accompanied by lots of sobbing nearly every day. Such periods often lasted for an hour or more. Once an inveterate reader, Carol temporarily lost her ability to concentrate while reading. She couldn't even focus on the articles in her adored gardening magazines.

The unfair difficulties endured throughout the criminal justice system had inflicted true psychological trauma on my wife. So Carol started seeing another therapist in the hope that it might help.

The stress was getting to me too. I could not believe what was happening to my wife, all because of a child's lies and the unscrupulous behavior of neighbors, and I started acting in uncharacteristic ways. Normally I'm a quiet, retiring individual, but I was becoming increasingly frustrated. One afternoon, when Butler (the anthesiologist who had called Carol a "Nazi") drove past me in my car, I gave him the finger. He stopped, backed up, and rolled down his passenger side window. I rolled down mine. He irately asked, "You got a problem?" I shot back, "Yeah, you called my wife a 'Nazi!'"

He answered back something to the effect that he did that, "….only after [your wife] got in my wife's face through the screened-in porch." Then he asked me if I wanted to fight. After I told him "no," he exclaimed, "If you want to fight, just flip me the bird one more time! Your wife is nuts and belongs in the crazy house." Then he drove off.

The exchange was unsettling, and I told Carol about it while we walked the dog a little later in the afternoon. I also said to her that I no longer wanted to live in our neighborhood; even if the Whites and Odoms were to move away one day, how could we enjoy our time there if our other neighbors held such attitudes?

Carol told me she never said anything to Butler's wife that day, although she had noticed his wife sitting on the porch with her husband.

The following day, Butler pulled up next to me while on his bicycle to apologize. He told me he was sorry for how the situation had developed, and indicated he had no ill will towards either my wife or me. I thanked him, and, without apologizing, told him I appreciated his comments. However, I explained that the whole thing mystified me; when had my wife upset his?

Butler told me Carol had an angry dispute one day with Tina White, during which his wife Stella had come to Tina's defense since the exchange was happening on his front lawn. At that time, Carol had "verbally assaulted" his wife.

When I spoke to Carol later, she said there had been no such encounter. Ultimately, we both concluded that Butler's 180-degree turnabout from his words of the previous day was significant, but we had no idea what motivated him.

Wear-and-Tear

Commuting back and forth from Visitors Inn, to home and back so that I could walk the dog and feed our cats, was wearing on me. Our dog and cats were getting less attention than they deserved, since no one was in the house in the late afternoons, evenings, and nights. I felt reduced to the roles of butler and chauffeur.

Moreover, this living in limbo was costing us a bundle: We were spending over $600 a week for the hotel, and $450 a week for Carol's chaperone. This was in addition to over $10,000 in out-of-pocket legal fees.

It was fortunate our insurance paid for Carol's involuntary commitment, as well as her meetings with her therapists and her psychiatrist, Dr. Kaczmarek.

Total Exile

At an April 27 hearing called on short order by the Judge, Self said he was sick of this case and banned Carol from 341 Pearly Lane, presumably until the time the case would be resolved. Root interjected that this was in lieu of going to jail.

Carol left court that day completely traumatized: It seemed inconceivable that she was now banned from even visits to her own home! Carol spoke to both her children about living with them temporarily, but it became clear that going to New Hampshire or Texas to stay with them would be problematic. Her daughter didn't want to deal with her, and her son had a scheduling problem. We decided then that we should go to New York City, where my sister lived. Much earlier — before this whole mess — we had purchased tickets so we could attend some operas there.

Carol managed to make it through the airline flight, but she was in a vulnerable state. When we reached my sister's place, Carol had difficulty making small talk, and excused herself to go upstairs. My sister and I could hear her up there sobbing. Carol recovered some by late afternoon, so we went to the opera.

Carol did okay during the first act, but started to feel uncomfortable in the second. She could not hold it together for the final act, and we left early to take a taxi back to my sister's.

My sister accurately classified Carol's emotional and psychological state as being very "fragile." She and I were convinced that Carol would not be able to withstand her gypsy, nomadic existence much longer without a nervous breakdown. We agreed that Carol should not remain in NYC for more than another day or two, and I bought new flight tickets so that Carol and I might return to Big Pebble as soon as possible.

New Developments

In May, Guildenstern informed us that William White would not allow him to question his son Willie. Our lawyer did tell us that he was still planning on interviewing Willie's friend, Tim Cutter — but when he did, we did not learn anything we didn't know already. And although Guildenstern told us he expected to interview several more kids from our neighborhood over the next few weeks, he never did.

Provocation

It was after dark during the second week of May when a group of about a dozen kids saw me getting into my car at our house after feeding our animals. They proceeded to almost hand-in-hand block my car's access to Laurel Avenue. I inched the car very slowly forward, and the kids moved aside.

One boy though jumped up and down in front of me to the right. I stopped the car for a second without saying anything or cracking my window. They either were trying to intentionally provoke me so that I would violate the no-contact order, or could say that I "attempted" to run one of them over.

I emailed Guildenstern about the incident. Two days later, Guildenstern reported the incident to Root. Shocking, the prosecutor told our lawyer that he had had a similar experience himself several blocks away the previous week! The kids seemed to have taken over our section of Big Pebble.

Unable to Bear It

On May 25, Carol sent Guildenstern an email asking him to request another hearing to let her back into our house. She provided our lawyer with a written statement to give to Root that read in part:

…Being banned from your house is like taking your life away, all that you love and care about. My husband has had to stop working, take sick leave in order to take care of me and our cats and dog (since I cannot)… This whole episode has cost us over $10,000 in legal fees and thousands more for hotels, apartments, and flights to places to stay away from home… As an overweight 71-year-old, I could not possibly pose a threat to any child except behind the wheel of a car, and I could be instead forbidden from driving in Sunken Valley.

… In my seventy–one years of life I never have been in conflict with the law, and I do not understand how the statement of one kid (corroborating statement by Odie Odom can be refuted by my husband) brought me such grief. This has shattered my faith in the entire criminal justice system in the U.S.

…I have had two children myself. I have successfully raised them and they are contributing members of this society. I never ever have in all my life had any problems or difficulties with children of any age… My house was always full of different children who came and went to interact with my children. Then all of a sudden at age 71, I should have developed scare tactics that the neighborhood children should be afraid of? Also, the kids showed no sign of fear of me after the incident, continuing to play basketball next door for many months.

My psychiatrist Dr. Kaczmarek and my counselor are willing to testify that I am a kind and caring person and there is absolutely no reason kids should be afraid of me.

When Guildenstern did not respond, I sent him a separate email. That communication read, in part:

- Carol originally had one court order forbidding contact with the Whites and the Boyles only. In January that was superseded by the order forbidding contact with anyone 16 and under.

- Despite pleas from me, you never did get the judge to define what was meant by no direct contact, and who was actually covered by his order... When I put the newspaper articles in Odom's mailbox and Tina White's windshield, I was read the riot act by Root and Self... even though I had not personally been included in any no contact order. At the courtroom, it became clear that from then on I was considered part of the no-contact order, again with nothing stipulated in writing.

- Now let me explain Carol's understanding of all this: a no-contact order from the judge means whatever the judge (and Root) want it to mean, that the rules get made up by them whenever it so pleases them. She understood that I now had to watch my step as well. I am convinced that she never understood what no direct contact meant...To a layman, particularly someone for whom English is not a native language, "no direct contact" means no physical contact, and could also be interpreted to mean no speech directed specifically at the other person, but not necessarily. In legal-ese, "no direct contact" clearly means something else, far more inclusive. This was never explained fully to Carol by the judge, by you or by me.

- Carol sometimes has problems figuring out certain things we might consider simple, despite her higher education. I kid her about that by saying it's because she doesn't have a Ph.D. One example is her failure to open up boxes and packages the way intended, despite her ability to figure out much more complex things.

- I have not seen the infamous video of Carol in the playground, but I think you could judge whether Carol's actions were consistent with the first (layman's) interpretation of "no direct contact" or not. I felt you could have assumed responsibility [at the hearing] for not having explained the definition of 'no direct contact' better.

While Guildenstern never responded to Carol's communication, he did to mine, telling me:

I understand what you are saying and I understand your position. What I recall saying, however, was that it means 'stay away from.' …The video shows her standing for approx. 15 minutes or so on or at the edge of the basketball court while the game — with all the various boys there — is going on around her. I have no problem with going to Self/Root again after a little more time has elapsed.

I don't know what Guildenstern intended with his email, but Carol was a bit bitter that Guildenstern had answered my email, and ignored hers.

Together, the two of us tried to hang on and survive in our "limbo" existence until something changed.

In Limbo and More Lawyers

We did want real change, so we looked into finding another lawyer — again.

Carol told me she would prefer a woman. I found Diana Fleming through the Yellow Pages. Flemming's ad attracted my attention because she was a former deputy prosecutor in town. That made me think she might have some good contacts in the prosecutor's office.

When we met with Diana Fleming, we liked her approach. Carol felt she could communicate with her better than with Guildenstern. The downside to hiring her was that Diana did appear to want to take our matter to a jury trial. Now, that would have been a very expensive proposition for us to fund. Additionally, and more importantly, both Carol and I thought it was unlikely that she would be able to endure the stress of a jury trial without experiencing a complete nervous breakdown.

The next day, I met with a lawyer seeking advice rather than representation. I had given the man an account of our story prior to the meeting.

At the meeting, the lawyer indicated that he personally knew William and Tina White, the Knights, prosecutor Root and Guildenstern. He told us that it was his impression that the forces arrayed against us were too strong, and would prove victorious at trial. When I asked why we wouldn't prevail, he looked down for a moment, then said quietly that he thought that Jeff Jefferson, the Chief Deputy Prosecutor for Big Pebble, lived on our street.

I was taken aback. *It suddenly became obvious how and why the prosecutor's office was in such lockstep with the Whites.* This news made my head reel.

The lawyer strongly advised that Carol and I sell our home and move. He made the point that we would have to endure the same neighbors in the future if Carol won at trial—meaning that at any time in the future, the neighborhood children could make another false accusation against us if there was an encounter. I hadn't really thought about this before, and the possibility created a sick sensation in my stomach.

The lawyer also agreed that he thought Carol's mental health would suffer if she tried to last through a jury trial.

The next day, Guildenstern called and indicated that Root had made an informal plea bargain offer to the effect that all Willie White-related charges would be dropped if Carol moved out of 341 Pearly Lane — permanently.

Throwing in the Towel

Three days later, we retained Diana Fleming. We told her of the "new" offer and about the Chief Deputy Prosecutor living so close to us. She indicated Jefferson had been her immediate supervisor, and commented that he was a "jerk." She said that his actions were clearly improper, and that we might want to see about getting a prosecutor from another county on our case.

I found the wife of Chief Deputy Prosecutor Jeff Jefferson on the Internet. She was a UEKMS Associate Professor. When I showed the information available on her to Carol, Carol recognized her face — and home. It was where one of the younger neighborhood boys playing in the intersection had run to one day.

Several days later, Diana Fleming informed us over the phone that our prosecutor had unofficially offered to drop all charges except leaving the scene of an accident if we agreed to sell our house and move. In a brusque tone, Diana told me that this was a "take it or leave it" situation.

She also said she had not spoken with Jefferson about his conflict of interest in our case, for she had decided that raising that issue and having it result in the appointment of a special prosecutor from another county would be counterproductive.

She sounded like Root's mouthpiece rather than our lawyer. Carol and I were not happy.

Although we had not yet formally accepted the plea deal, we house-hunted over the next few days, resigned to the fact that we would be forced out of our home for good. Carol and I felt it was best to buy a new house first before selling our Pearly Lane house; otherwise, we'd have difficulty finding a temporary place that would accept our dog and three cats. After Carol picked out a house that she liked, I insisted she meet some of the neighbors in order to ensure that we would not run into problems such as we encountered with the Whites and Odoms.

She did as I suggested. She liked the neighbors she informally spoke with, and discovered that there were far fewer children in this neighborhood than at Pearly Lane.

On June 24, we signed a contract on the house many miles from Sunken Valley.

The next day, we told our lawyer the news. She indicated our signing of the contract should satisfy Root, and the fact that we were waiting to list our home until we could move our animals to our new house shouldn't be a problem. Then, to our dismay, Diana asked if there were any kids in the new neighborhood.

We could not understand how the prosecutor could suddenly insist on such a thing! If we sold our home at 341 Pearly Lane, all charges against Carol were to be dropped except for leaving the scene of an accident! The prosecutor's office should not be able to restrict where we bought our new house.

Diana called the prosecutor's office, and after the conversation indicated to us that Root, the prosecutor, was satisfied about hearing of our upcoming move to the house we intended to purchase.

At the end of June, I began weekly therapy sessions myself. I was feeling extremely bitter about the situation that had befallen us, and the complete lack of support we had encountered from both our neighbors and the institution where I worked. On top of that, my work had suffered greatly because taking care of Carol and our animals had become a nearly full-time responsibility. The therapy seemed to help.

A Potential Close to the Case

Root sent a letter to our lawyer indicating that if we moved to the new house, Carol's criminal mischief charge would be reduced to a misdemeanor resulting in a $250 fine, court costs, and one year of probation with counseling continued until deemed unnecessary by Carol's counselor.

The aggravated assault charge would not be prosecuted subject to three provisions, one of which stated that, "…this charge could be re-filed in the event that there are any similar problems during the probationary period."

The letter also said that our prior lawyer had initiated the request for such an arrangement — whereas in reality it was the prosecutor who had suggested this arrangement initially, and several times thereafter.

Over the next week and a half, Carol and I asked our lawyer for explanations of several matters in the letter, but Diana did not answer us. Frustrated by Diana Fleming's complete lack of response to the questions the prosecutor's letter raised, Carol fired her and re-hired Guildenstern. He promptly explained those issues in Root's letter that we did not fully comprehend.

Two days later, Diana Fleming telephoned Carol, told her she never received our emails or telephone calls, and further indicated that she intended to keep our entire $5,000 retainer because she "negotiated" the plea bargain with Root. This was not the case, since she had earlier told us we had to accept "…whatever Root was offering."

Even Guildenstern was taken aback by Fleming's representation of the story.

By July 22, we moved most of our furnishings and belongings to our new house. *Might our awful, long ordeal finally be coming to an end?*

There was a July 27 hearing, held in response to our moving. This day, Root waived most charges, so that Carol would be on one year of probation for misdemeanor criminal mischief; $250 fine and court costs for leaving scene of an accident; and possible re-instatement of aggravated assault charges if any other similar incidents occur.

After the hearing was over, Root met with Carol in the probation office of the courthouse. He said he was sorry about what had happened to her. He told her that it "…should not have happened," but that the circumstances were such that he needed to do what he did, and that he was awfully sorry and hoped that this would not have continuing ill effects on her life.

Guildenstern witnessed this encounter and conversation, telling us afterward that for a prosecutor to choose to do this was "…extremely rare."

The next day, an *East Kansas Republic-Tribune* headline indicated that Carol moved to avoid conviction. This was not the case.

We moved because we wanted to prevent Carol from having a complete nervous breakdown, and because we couldn't sustain the "in limbo" lifestyle imposed upon us.

She wasn't guilty, and even the fact that the Prosecutor was willing to inflict her on a naïve new neighborhood clearly indicated he didn't believe she was the homicidal maniac he was portraying her.

CHAPTER 8: EPILOGUE: GETTING AWAY FROM IT ALL? NOT REALLY.

Aside from the costs of having to move to a new house, Carol and I found the loss of our home at 341 Pearly Lane especially devastating. I had chosen the place for its first-floor master bedroom, since Carol had experienced a long rehabilitation in Galveston after breaking her leg. The bedroom and other rooms in the back of the house also had a view out to a yard that we had fashioned into a spectacular backyard garden — something that I felt might help Carol let go of our beloved home of twenty-two years in Galveston.

We fully expected to live out the rest of our years there. Losing this home, especially under the specific circumstances that transpired, was horrific.

Another fall-out from our battle with the criminal justice system was the loss of our cherished lifestyle. It was a major lifestyle change to have to drive to work from our new home. For my entire thirty-plus year's career as a faculty member, I had managed to live within walking distance of work. It was a lifestyle I highly valued, and took great pains to maintain. By living so close, I was able to get just the right amount of exercise through walking to and from work, and walking back and forth for lunch. I have always hated commuting, and was proud to conserve gasoline. Moreover, living in our Pearly Lane home permitted my wife and me to share just one car.

Lastly, while any kind of moving is stressful, moving against one's will is even more so. Too, the response of our Sunken Valley neighbors to our situation was especially disappointing. Many were convinced that the allegations leveled against Carol were true. Others who knew better chose not to get involved, or even to maintain relations. Moreover, the garden clubs to which Carol belonged had disinvited her from their meetings because of the case leveled against her.

Everyone expected Carol's mood to improve upon our move, but her mood and depression actually got worse. She started developing abdominal cramping followed by severe nausea. She became very afraid of remaining at our new home alone, or of being on the upstairs level even if I was there with her. She did not sleep well, and periodically asked whether we would be able to buy back 341 Pearly Lane.

At Carol's probation meetings, she felt the officers treated her like a criminal. Too, the presence of some unsavory-looking individuals waiting to meet with their probation officers frightened her. I must admit, many of these people looked so disreputable that I was nervous myself while waiting for her in the parking lot (I was not allowed to accompany her inside).

Dr. Kaczmarek changed Carol's medication mix to increase the anti-anxiety properties. This brought Carol a measure of relief, but she was still suffering greatly from her ordeal.

Since I could no longer walk to work, we had to buy a second car.

On the legal front, Diana Fleming refunded us $1,000 of the $5,000 retainer after we indicated we were prepared to bring the matter to the attention of the Office of Professional Conduct, Supreme Court of East Kansas.

During September and October, Carol's depression worsened. She managed to exercise most days, but was unable to focus on her former favorite activities of gardening and reading. She was fearful too of going outside in our new, less-populated neighborhood. She cried nearly every morning when I left the house to go to work.

Meanwhile, late in August, the Butlers sold their house and moved out of Sunken Valley. On October 1, the Odoms moved to Massachusetts. At the end of the month, Tina White and her three kids moved to Florida, leaving the man she had divorced, William White, to reoccupy 340 Pearly Lane.

In November, Carol was nauseous every morning, and on some days, all day long. She was diagnosed with stress-induced gastritis or an ulcer. At the probation office, she had to provide a urine sample while the officers watched.

Nothing in her case ever suggested a need for a drug screening at any time.

Since the neighborhood children primarily involved in our case had left Big Pebble, at our request Guildenstern asked Root if he would consider shortening Carol's probation, or letting us move back into 341 Pearly Lane. Our old home was listed for sale, but still unsold. Root's answer: NO WAY.

Coping with Carol's downward emotional spiral was difficult for me. On a temporary basis, I began weekly meetings with a social worker therapist of the UEKMS Employee Assistance Program. She recommended Carol meet with a therapist regarding a new form of therapy (eye movement desensitization and reprocessing, EMDR) especially useful for post-traumatic stress, but that didn't seem to help. I took Carol to a session with a hypnotherapist; she did not find the visit useful.

Over the course of several sessions in December, my therapist recommended several books. I recommended the two I found particularly helpful — Eckhart Tolle's *The Power of Now* and Martin Seligman's *Learned Optimism* — to Carol, but they didn't help her as much as they had helped me.

After Carol's son and his girlfriend spent Christmas with us, Carol's spirits picked up. Her nausea subsided.

However, I was having my difficulties at work. As a sixty-year-old full professor, I had to move my lab and office into smaller quarters. I had to recruit paid help to move the heaviest items, as only two people in the department offered to help. I lost both my employees, and for a year, had to shutter my laboratory.

2010

In January, I began sessions with a new therapist to whom I related well.

Our Pearly Lane home had not sold yet. Any Open Houses often were marked by the appearance of neighborhood children, who would mischievously ask the prospective buyers "…if they knew who the owners were."

In February, Carol asked for permission for her to visit our house at Pearly Lane because of our difficulties in selling it. She received it a month later, provided she visited only during school hours on weekdays in the company of a chaperone who was not a family member.

When Carol and her chaperone went to our old home, she was surprised by her negative reaction to the sight of our old neighborhood. She made up her mind she wanted to sell the house as quickly as possible.

We dropped the listing price by $10,000, and when nothing transpired, dropped it another $20,000.

In July, we reduced the listing price by yet another $10,000. In mid-August, our Pearly Lane home finally sold, but for approximately $50,000 less than we paid, not to mention what we spent on upgrades.

We were drained financially. We had had to support two mortgages for a whole year until the Pearly Lane house sold, and our second mortgage was now larger than the first due to our lack of equity.

At this point, our legal and other costs stemming from this incident were astronomical:

- Out-of-pocket legal fees for attorneys: over $15,000.
- $9,000 out-of-pocket expenses for psychiatric and counseling help (fortunately, our insurance mostly paid the expenses for involuntary and forced commitments).
- $6,000 in temporary housing costs.
- $36,000 due to having to cover a mortgage and utility payments for a second home; this went on for a full year until we were able to sell until our first home.
- $2,500 to "stage" our Pearly Lane house in order to try to sell it faster.
- $20,000 for the realtor's 6% commission and closing costs.
- An additional $70,000 for our new home (when compared to the price we paid for our Pearly Lane home). The mortgage payments on our new home for a year were to prove much more due to our new lack of equity.
- $35,000 for a second car that had not been needed when we lived in walking distance of work.

In sum, these costs approached $200,000. *We would not have been able to meet our ongoing monthly bills were it not for an inheritance from my grandfather.* But even this inheritance did not last long, with the result being that our savings ended up being totally depleted.

Carol and I unfortunately discovered that both the direct and incidental costs of mounting a defense once one is targeted by the criminal justice system could be enormous — even if one is innocent. It is a burden few can absorb without suffering major trauma that can affect all aspects of one's life, including one's lifestyle, relationships, health, and more.

In September, we were able to refinance our new home using the equity from the sale of our Pearly Lane house.

In November, after a very long session with Dr. Kaczmarek, Carol was diagnosed as severely depressed and in need of higher dosages of antidepressant meds. We visited my cousin in Houston over Thanksgiving; it was a nice break, but Carol still hadn't recovered from her ordeal.

2011

I was able to revive my laboratory in early 2011, although I had to start "from scratch" with entirely new personnel, something very difficult to do. I have never had to do this before in my entire scientific career.

At the beginning of February, against the specific advice of Guildenstern, Carol called Judge Self's office, who told her that her file had been expunged (sealed) on October 6, 2010. We were relieved.

2012

By February, Carol had been slowly improving. On the week before the Flower and Garden Show at the end of the month, she showed an enthusiasm for entering some plants and arrangements that I hadn't seen in years, and I encouraged her. The day before the show, I dropped off Carol with her entries for the Flower and Garden Show at the Convention Center and left. She stayed to catalog and fill out her entries. When she was done, she presented this to a woman who promptly asked her "Aren't you the woman who tried to run over that little boy?" Carol was totally devastated by this lightning bolt out of the blue.

Anguished, I brought our story to Jim Larson, author of the *Republic-Tribune* articles about Carol. He was very cordial. He indicated to me that he had been pleased to write articles about a case that had a positive outcome. I was stunned. A week later, I emailed him and asked, "Do you still feel this had a good outcome for us? Do you think justice was served?"

Mr. Larson responded: "I'm sorry that this had been an ordeal for you and your wife, but I don't think the newspaper can help you. The only place I know in our society that you can get the remedy you appear to be seeking is the courts. In my meager opinion, any defendant who can walk freely out of a courtroom and obtain a clear criminal record has gotten the best outcome available. For your second question, after more than 20 years as a reporter, I would not presume to tell anyone whether they have received justice."

Wow, were we taken aback by this commentary on the system!

That year, we also had to endure the ordeal of encountering hundreds of Root for Judge signs all over town both for an initial election in the spring and for a run-off in November. We couldn't seem to escape what he had done to us. Fortunately, from our point of view, he lost the run-off.

CHAPTER 9: THE AFTERMATH TO THE "PERFECT STORM"

In sum, our experiences as individuals and a family since the case was closed is summarized as follows: Carol went into another downward psychological spiral after we moved, and required much therapy and medication to cope with the trauma of what had befallen her. Although her state of mind has improved over the years since, the process has been agonizingly slow. It remains to be seen whether she will ever fully regain her former self.

These developments have been extremely disconcerting for me as well. I remain profoundly ashamed of my inability to protect or defend Carol from these injuries and injustices. Unquestionably, 2008-2010 were the worst years in Carol's life and in mine as well.

I began to turn a corner in mid-2010, but not Carol and I can't hold her responsible: The legal system appeared rigged against her, and I hold mean-spirited former neighbors and the criminal justice system as responsible.

What we endured was the result of actions by people whom we knew and worked or lived with in our community. We faced variously mean-spirited and irresponsible parents, as well as neighbors who were completely apathetic to our situation. We found it extremely surprising to encounter the kind of complicity we did between our neighbors and the justice system in a fair-sized city. Our experience in living through this Kafka-esque ordeal made us rage against the system that oppressed us, and express our anguish about those around us who failed to assist us.

Carol and I have found it so very difficult to come to terms with our experiences, for we live in a society that prides itself on the opposite: being altruistic and reaching out to help those in need. Imagine, too, the object lessons learned by the kids involved after they successfully duped their own parents into carrying out a vendetta on an elderly woman.

In the 2009 words of the then chief psychiatrist at UEKMS, Carol and I were caught in "a perfect storm," in which all the forces — in our neighborhood, in the criminal justice system, and in the media — aligned against us.

Because of everything that had happened, Carol and I came to hate the criminal justice and legal systems. Even though we still live here, we are not fond of Big Pebble.

I am glad that my father passed away in 2008 without having to witness the fate that has befallen us here.

The Motivation for Writing This Book

Together, Carol and I decided to write this book in the hope that offering up what we learned from our ordeal may spare others a similar fate. We certainly made our share of mistakes, but none that deserved the trauma we endured. Initially we believed that our experience was some horrible peculiarity of the criminal justice system in Big Pebble.

It was not, is not. *For those of you who have read this far and feel that nothing like this will happen to you, watch out!* As we looked into the workings of the U.S. criminal justice system more generally, we found out countless others have suffered far worse than we did. Discovering and reading about the suffering of so many others led us to uncover horrendous flaws in the system, and then to generate suggestions to overhaul the system.

Through this book, Carol and I hope to generate something positive out of all the negativity that we endured.

It is unwise for others to remain as naïve or ignorant as we were with respect to how the justice system, legal system, and community can impact a person in adverse and completely unexpected ways.

We have changed the names of all participants in our saga to disguise their identities, since we are not out for revenge. But we felt it essential to disclose many of the myriad details of our case to you, the reader, to present you with a real picture of what can occur if you are unprepared and naïve about the judicial process in our country. Rather than have you learn the hard way as we did, we want to use our experience to describe what we did wrong out of ignorance, what we've learned since, and how the system can be improved based upon our experiences. Thus, the second part of the book represents our thoughts on what is wrong with different parts of the system, and how they might be improved.

So we beg you to please read on. True justice in our nation depends on it.

PART II

CHAPTER 10: WHEN AND WHY KIDS LIE

When a lie that any child creates puts us — a beloved friend, a family member, a valued neighbor, or our own children — at risk, it is painful. It's hard to maintain objectivity, or figure out the motivation behind the lie.

Some of us may take a step back or not initially treat an allegation seriously if a minor is involved—but that is the completely wrong approach *if it means failing to protect yourself or your loved one adequately right from the start.* If the lie(s) is serious in nature, consider it carefully, and respond to it thoughtfully. In Carol's and my experience, children who were lying were treated with "kid gloves" by the authorities — and even by the lawyers.

In my situation, a child's lie traumatized my significant other; destroyed our marital home and lifestyle; blew up our finances and ability to retire comfortably in the near future; and ultimately put my job at risk. So let me give you the benefit of my and Carol's hindsight on the importance of considering the backdrop of a juvenile's lie. *When and why do kids lie, and how does a tendency to lie develop in a child?*

How Lying Develops in Kids

According to researchers, children begin to lie as soon as their consciousness develops to the point where they can talk and/or understand what adults are saying—and that is around age two years of age. Commonly, toddlers lie to deny they have done something wrong (often pointing out someone else as the culprit: "Johnny did it!"), or to acquire something they want for themselves (a beloved rocking horse; a toy puppet).[1]

From ages two to five, children often lie because they do not think what they did was wrong. Or, an active imagination leads them to think any "imaginary friends" and other such characters are real, leading them to attribute a forbidden or harmful act to them. For example, a two-year-old may pull the tail of a cat, and when asked about this, might say an imaginary friend, "Princess Elsa," did it.

Preschoolers also may lie because they want something they are not supposed to have, such as an extra piece of pie for dessert. So they may tell their grandmother that their mother told them "…it is okay" for them to have it. As researcher Juliette Guilbert says, "Preschoolers' tall tales can be pure play, or sometimes wishful thinking…It's not unusual for young kids to insist…that their fantasy world is real."[2]

But as their consciousness of other people develops, children experience different motivations to lie. From age five to eight, kids may engage in white lies to benefit someone else or avoid hurting someone's feelings — a pattern that can continue into the later teen years and adulthood. Some other reasons kids might lie at this age include the desire to not disappoint someone ("But Billy expected me to win the race."); to escape getting punished; or to avoid something they are asked to do that is beyond their abilities ("I also can do ten pull-ups, just not today because I hurt my fingers playing ball earlier!").

When children become adolescent or teenagers and start to yearn for independence, they place extraordinary value on their peers and peer groups. They become secretive about their lives, deliberately concealing information from their parents ("No, there's only going to be girls at the party; no boys are invited.") and experiencing a desire to impress their peers ("I'm doing so well at swimming that I'm probably going to make the swim team!"). They may exaggerate, embellish the truth, or totally fabricate a story to make life more interesting and in order to receive more attention, love, and/or approval.[3]

Young adolescent males typically are inspired by action heroes in movies; those characters that gain prestige and honor for feats of daring and who often employ lying and trickery to escape a villain. So they themselves become inclined to apply a similar approach in order to "pump up" the excitement in their own humdrum everyday lives. Both children and adolescents can "…tell elaborate stories which appear believable," often relating them with a great deal of enthusiasm, because "they receive a lot of attention as they tell the lie." [4]

Kids also lie to protect somebody else, or out of loyalty to a friend. Loyalty among teenagers can be so strong it becomes "like a code of ethics for them," and they consider it a "breach of friendship to rat on their friends." [5]

Additionally, lying to gain some kind of advantage or avoid some kind of punishment is more prevalent if kids are under stress or receiving a lack of parental controls that can happen when a divorce is happening in a family. It's common for kids to "act out" when their family life undergoes significant changes.[2]

And once they've lied, why don't they eventually "come clean" so that the lie doesn't plague their conscience? Many children are fearful of admitting to their lies: They want to "avoid facing the music" — or the punishment they might receive from, say, parents, teachers, or coaches.[6]

When there are Serious Reasons Prompting the Lies

Revenge

Kids may lie out of their desire to seek revenge. (Of course, this is true of some adults as well. In the lyrics to the popular Carrie Underwood song, "Before He Cheats," a girlfriend who has been cheated on admits to slashing the tires on her boyfriend's car, and swinging a Louisville Slugger bat into that vehicle's headlights.)

Although this reason is less common for kids, its existence speaks to the popularity of revenge and lying in our culture as a way to solve problems. This approach can be seen especially in TV shows and films where revenge is justified and/or glorified as a way to "get back" at somebody who has wronged someone else. Given the power of media today, children and teenagers are heavily influenced to engage in acts of revenge, just like their role models or adored celebrities in the movies and on TV.

Reality shows such as *Big Brother*, *Real Housewives*, *Amazing Race*, and *Survivor*, all feature people who are not above resorting to revenge to avenge a perceived wrong. These popular post-2000 movies glamorize revenge: "a harmful action against a person or group in response to a grievance, real or perceived, [which] is also called retribution, retaliation, vengeance, or 'payback'": *Gladiator*, *The Dark Knight*, *Kill Bill*, *I Spit on Your Grave*, *Batman: Under the Red Hood*, *Taken*, *V for Vendetta*, *Seven Days*, *The Brave One*, *Mean Creek*, *Hobo with a Shotgun*, *Four Brothers*, *Machete*, and *The Girl with the Dragon Tattoo*.[7] In these movies, the protagonists choose revenge as an appropriate strategy for getting back at someone they feel wronged them, whereby the protagonists typically engage in lying, trickery, and/or deceit to further their plot.

If a person or group humiliates a child in some way, it can also fill that child with the desire to seek revenge. Psychologist Julie Fitness points to a link between the two, citing that humiliation "…inflicts such a deep and painful injury to a person's self-esteem and social status, taking revenge might well be regarded as a powerful means of restoring dignity and regaining some control over the situation."[8]

Cases of Physical or Sexual Abuse

When kids claim they have been physically abused in some way, authorities react seriously to the charge. In fact, generally the initial reaction by police, prosecutors, and the media is to proceed as if the accusation is true, despite the legal presumption of innocent until proven guilty. This makes any false accusations much more difficult to refute.

Recently, for example, *The New York Daily News* reported on an Alabama assistant principal who lost her job due to allegations of sexual abuse by a student. The principal resigned after the school district suspended her, and due to the pressure of the allegations. Police then charged her. By the time the student recanted and admitted his story was a lie, the assistant principal, who had been unable to find another job, had been forced to sell her house and move back in with her mother. [9]

Carol's case was especially problematic because *only rarely are adults other than parents, relatives of a child, or teachers accused of physical abuse.* If the child's accusation involves a family member or relative, social workers or child protective services usually form the first line of response. These "initial responders" analyze the situation and determine if the child was telling the truth — and, if so, whether the minor should be removed from the home environment. But even then, the police might not be contacted since once the child was out of the home the first responders usually go on to further investigate the case.

In the case of accused teachers or other school officials (like the Alabama principal), the first line of response is performed by school counselors, then by school officials or the district. Here too, the police might not become involved at all unless they felt the accusation had weight.

However, once a child's accusation involves any other type of adult, such as a babysitter or a neighbor, the complaint is handled within the criminal justice system. Unfortunately (and as Carol and I found out for ourselves), the police and prosecutors often do not possess the necessary training to carefully and/or properly assess such claims to establish their truth before a case is argued in a court of law.

And once the media or Internet get ahold of such a claim, inevitably the public becomes biased against the alleged perpetrator. Even if the claim is later shown to be false, the alleged abuser may have already suffered job suspension (often without pay, as in the case of the Alabama assistant principal); loss of clients (if he/she owns a business); and isolation from friends, business associates, and even family members. As a result, a falsely accused abuser can become isolated and very vulnerable, lacking in both financial and emotional support during an extremely trying time

Yet not only are a vast number of child abuse claims made each year, but a high number of them are found to be false. In 2010, 2.98 million children in the United States underwent a Child Protective Services investigation for an allegation of child abuse or neglect, with 2-10% of the child abuse claims found to be false. This means 60,000-300,000 children were involved in a false child abuse claim that year. In child custody disputes, false allegation rates skyrocket to as high as 36-55%.[10]

Why such high false child abuse claims? In alleged physical abuse cases, the National Child Abuse Defense and Resource Center note there is rarely a search for an "equally competing hypothesis" for causation of any injuries. The presumption is that the injury or injuries were non-accidental — and therefore must have been inflicted by someone. The Stop Abusive and Violent Environments website reports that there is a lack of presumption of innocence.[11]

Yet the result of any presumption of truth telling by a child when the case is being handled in the criminal justice system is that the person accused of the abuse must prove their innocence, as the child is assumed to have told the truth. Only if the child can quickly be shown to be lying — such as by bringing in a witness to contradict false testimony — can damage to an innocent person be contained.

Perjury in Criminal Cases

While perjury is considered a very serious crime and is classified as a felony with the possibility of a long prison term of up to five years, it can be very hard to prove it in a criminal case — even when a jury disbelieves the testimony in the original trial. Consequently, there are very few perjury trials.

Legally, perjury is defined as "the willful giving of a false testimony under oath." However, the lie must *be relevant to the case itself* to be considered perjury, or it will not be considered as such. The lie has to "have the potential to affect the outcome of the proceedings."[12] For example, if a person lies about their age, number of kids, or marital status, it may not be perjury if such testimony does not directly affect the outcome of the case.

It is also necessary to prove that the individual telling a lie actually *intended* to do so, and did not simply make a mistake, misunderstand the question, or recall something incorrectly. Consequently, very few perjury cases are filed. Even when prosecutors are aware that defendants and witnesses are lying, they generally do not seek to prosecute them. As one long-time prosecutor told Suro and Miller, "There's lying in criminal cases all the time… defendants lie. They bring in alibi witnesses who lie. But we usually will not prosecute them for perjury." The prosecutors will not prosecute witnesses who perjure themselves to help them make the prosecutors' case against a defendant.

Another problem with prosecuting a perjury case is that a person can make a misleading statement or answer a question with a statement that is true but doesn't answer the question, thereby concealing the lie. In effect, the person is lying through the "literal truth defense." In the U.S. Supreme Court in *Bronston v. United States* (409 U.S. 352, 353 (1973)), the issue was whether a witness could be "convicted of perjury for an answer, under oath, that is literally true but not responsive to the question asked and arguably misleading by negative implication."[13] In the case, when Bronston was asked if *he* ever had any bank accounts in Swiss banks, he replied, "…the company had an account there for about six months in Zurich." What he failed to disclose was that he had a large personal bank account there! The Supreme Court reversed his original conviction of perjury (which had been on the grounds that in an ordinary conversation his response would probably be understood to imply that he never had a personal bank account there), as in court, what mattered was what he actually *stated,* not what he *implied.* Bronston had literally stated the truth and the examining lawyer had to probe deeper and clarify the response, should a witness give a vague or misleading response.

One famous example of this difficulty of proving perjury charges is the 1998 Clinton impeachment hearing case where Clinton repeatedly gave evasive answers about his sexual involvement with then-White House intern Monica Lewinsky. For example, when asked how often he and Ms. Lewinsky were alone in the Oval Office, he initially stated he did not recall, but later added, "It seems to me she brought things to me once or twice on the weekends. In that case, whatever time she would be in there, drop it off, exchange a few words and go." While that statement was literally true, Clinton later admitted to the two of them being alone ten to fifteen times. So his initial statement was literally true — although misleading-and it was successfully used in his defense.[13]

In summary, *if you or someone significant to you is charged in a criminal case, never assume any witness will be obliged to tell the truth.* Saving yourself or your loved one from jail or probation rests on *you* — and perhaps your lawyer or other legal defense team. *Do all that you can to introduce the facts that will support your version of events!* You will never regret the time, effort, and expense spent.

That advice given, let's look at how we can work to prevent or stop children from lying, both as parents and as a society.

HOW TO DO IT BETTER

Given that all kids lie to some extent (as do all adults), what can parents do to prevent or stop their kids from lying — especially those very serious and harmful lies that not only hurt others, but potentially ruin lives?

First, *parents need to first recognize the possibility that children do in fact lie—not only to others, but to themselves.* Yet many parents do not want to acknowledge either possibility. In Carol's case, neither Tina White nor Brody Odom would consider the possibility their son was lying to them. In fact, Tina stated flatly to Carol that her son "would never lie" to her. Moreover, Brody Odom was a social worker specializing in adolescent psychology, but he never acted as if there was the remotest possibility his son was lying.

Then, when I put an article on their property to remind them that kids do in fact lie, they reacted with anger and denial to the possibility. They treated my behavior as a personal attack against them as a way to retaliate against Willie's claims against my wife.

As Parents

We may adore our children, but that doesn't mean they are perfect. We see it all the time, through their unruly behavior and their failure to go to bed on time, study as they need to, and abide by some household rules. They don't have the wisdom of experience, and the choices available to them in today's world can be confusing. We are not our child's best friend, but we are their parents. *As their parents, we need to offer our children help and guidance as we raise them, and we need to impart values we think are right, such as truth telling.*

To best help our children, we need to recognize that all kids, at one point or another, in their lives lie — just as we undoubtedly did while growing up. Then, if we do suspect our child has engaged in a lie, we need to keep control of our anger or disappointment, and carefully handle the situation, even if the lie is extremely upsetting. Here are some suggestions from a host of leading childcare experts about how to short-circuit, handle, and prevent lying in children:

- *Cool down yourself before you try to do anything about a child's lying.* As psychologist Hartwell-Walker describes it, "Are you pretty sure your kid lied to you? Before dealing with it, go to your happy place. Breathe. Count. Pray. Are you calm now? Ok. Now talk to the kid." The adage, "Take a deep breath and count to ten," applies here. [3]

- *If you suspect a child is lying about a serious matter, create a safe space so your child can feel free to talk to you.* Don't use scare tactics or cross-examine your child if you suspect dishonesty or deliberate concealment.

- *Do not trap your child into a lie when they have misbehaved, such as by creating a "no-win" situation or using leading questions.* For example, if your child comes home with a black eye, don't greet them with, "I will really be furious if you got into a fight. Did you get into a fight today?" Here you are creating a situation where your child has to tell the truth and face your anger — or otherwise lie to avoid your anger by providing you with an alternative explanation. A better approach would be to ask what happened and invite the child to sit down to talk about it. [14] ("Ryan, I see that you have a black eye. Let's sit down and talk about what happened so that we can make sure you don't get into a situation like this again in the future.")

- *Avoid labeling a child as a "liar" as opposed to calling him out on their behavior.* Labeling a child "a liar" negatively undermines that juvenile's self-esteem — and research shows this could lead to even more lying. So stop judging, maintain your cool, and focus on correcting your child's actions and behaviors. [15]

- *Have a serious talk with your child about lying.* Stop believing the lies, and look for the reasons underlying them, so that you can talk about them.[16]
- *Know that lying is a learned but changeable behavior.* Children learn — from us and their other caregivers; from their friends; and as we've shown, even from the character they watch on TV or in their favorite movies. It doesn't really matter whom they picked up the behavior from; what matters is to stop this learned behavior in its tracks, as efficiently as possible. A great way to do this is to create negative consequences so the child realizes it isn't okay to lie. For example, tell your child if they lie again about who started the sibling fight, they are going to be separated from their sibling for the next fifteen minutes and have to play on their own by themselves. If your child is older, tell them that if they lie about where they went and what they did with their friends, you are no longer going to allow them to hang out with those friends.[6]
- *Do not accept their excuses or reasons for lying.* Sometimes, this is a tough piece of advice to abide by. But even if something good came out of the lie, you need to have a straightforward, earnest talk with the child that it is better to live without a certain outcome than to achieve a goal by lying about it.
- *Don't make lying a moral issue — make it a technical issue of breaking the rules.* As Lehman puts it: "Just be clear. Lying is wrong, it's hurtful, and, in our home, we tell the truth... You broke the law. You broke the rules. These are the consequences." When you're simple, impartial, and yet authoritative, it is easier on your child because you are giving them a clear blueprint to follow. In some ways, it is like how teachers are supposed to handle it at school.[17]
- *Create predictable consequences for telling a lie.* For example: Tell your teen that if they lie to their friend about another child liking them, then that teen is going to feel humiliated when they find out the truth one day. Tell your preschooler that if they lie about stealing their friend's toy, it hurts both of them.[6]
- *Enforce your own rules and punishments for lying.* If you threaten a punishment, it cannot be an idle threat — *you must carry through.* For example, tell your three-to-five-year-old that if they tell a lie, they're going to have to sit in the time-out corner. Then make sure this happens the next time they lie! Advise your six-to-

twelve-year-old that if they tell a lie, they are going to have to approach the person they lied to, admit to the lie, and then apologize. Then make sure this happens the next time they lie! Inform your adolescent or teen child that if they lie, they are going to have to admit to it, apologize, and offer to do something (rake the neighbor's yard; pay for the window they broke by throwing the ball) to "make up" for the untruth.[6]

- *Increase the severity of the consequences with each lie and distinguish the consequences for lying from the incident itself.* As James Lehman, a renowned child behavior therapist, suggests, a parent might say something like this: "The first time you lie, you go to bed an hour early. The second time, you lose your cell phone privileges," or "If you come home later than your curfew and you tell me the truth, you may still lose going out Friday night, but you won't lose your phone. If you lie to me about it, you lose both."[17]

- *Provide fair punishments for lying or doing anything else that is wrong.* Sometimes we too are a bit misguided: In our efforts to set and keep our child on the right path in life, we may instill parental consequences that are too harsh. For example, we might ground our child for a month if they lie about visiting a website we have restricted. This can lead a child to lie to avoid a punishment that they feel is unfair. It is better to discuss the situation with your child, then instill a punishment that is fair and in keeping with their age, stepping up the punishment only if the child does not change their behavior, One might say, for example, "Honey, we asked you not to visit that website because some of the material on it is not appropriate and too violent for a child your age. Since you did so and then lied to us about it, you have lost computer privileges for a week. If you continue to visit that website or any other one we have told you not to, we are going to initiate parental controls on the computer that are going to keep you from accessing a lot of sites that you enjoy and otherwise would be perfectly acceptable to us."[18]

- *Recognize that children often lie to keep their parents and teachers happy, so let your children know that you value their telling the truth "...much more than a small act of misbehavior."* The desire to keep parents happy is the kind of motivation that leads kids to lie about how well they are doing in school, so they may claim their grades are higher than they are. In this case, *you want to show you appreciate however well your child is doing so long they are doing the best job possible for them.* Explain that you would much rather they get a lower grade than to cheat or lie to make it appear they got a higher one.[19]

- *Praise truth-telling, and let your child know how much you value it at a time when a child might be tempted to lie but doesn't.*[19]
- *Look for any positive intent behind a lie and show you understand the child's reasons, but offer an example of what to do instead.*[20]
- *Avoid 'little white lies,' and role-play "the potential devastating consequences of lying."*[19]
- *If lying is a habit, talk with your child calmly about the pattern of behavior.* For example, talk about how lying makes you feel, explaining that it undermines your relationship with them. Bring up the consequences for continued lying.[15]
- *Become a better role model for honesty yourself.*

As a Society

Let's tackle the more general issue of short-circuiting a child's tendency to lie as they grow up.

- *From idea writer Gini Graham Scott's* The Truth About Lying: *Require children to take a Lie-Q Test.*
- After their scores are graded, they could be placed in classes or workshop programs for others with a similar score to discuss how and why they lie as well as why they should use other behaviors instead of lying. Alternatively, any children and teens who score especially high in lying might be required to participate in counseling, to help the children see what may be motivating them to lie, and to address these issues.[21]
- *Schools (both pre-school and grade), religious institutions that offer Sunday-school-type programs, and homeschoolers should encourage role-playing experiences in which children experience both sides of the story: lying to someone else and being lied to.* Then the children could be shown better alternatives, and given a chance to role-play these as well.
- *When a juvenile makes an accusation in a criminal case, a child psychologist specially trained in prosecutorial questioning as well as in false accusations and confessions should interview the child*

to determine if they are lying. This psychologist should meet with both prosecutor and defense attorney beforehand to be advised of specific matters to try to ascertain pertinent to the case at hand. (It is not practical or fair to have a child interviewed by multiple adults with different agendas and biases.)

Such questioning should occur in a comfortable environment where children and teens can feel relaxed and supported, *as opposed to the traditional interview room generally used by police and prosecutors.* After the interview, the psychologist should make a full report of it, along with recommendations regarding the veracity of the child's statements. It may also be advisable to videotape such interviews for possible use by either prosecutors or defense attorneys, perhaps instead of putting the child on the witness stand.

CHAPTER 11: ABUSES OF INVOLUNTARY COMMITMENTS

Our mental health system can be a saving grace: Some people voluntarily turn to the system if they experience serious emotional and mental problems. Then there are provisions on city, county, and state levels to render involuntary commitments under certain circumstances, to protect both the individual and the community at large.

Involuntary commitment is a *civil* commitment, so it is processed through the regular court system rather than criminal courts. It is meant to address those with symptoms of a severe mental illness that have also been deemed as sufficiently disturbed to harm themselves or others. Commonly, this kind of commitment is used in cases where an individual is schizophrenic, paranoid, delusional, psychotic, or otherwise exhibits signs of seriously disturbed behavior. Moreover, there is generally a clear indication such persons need help for self-protection — for instance, they are suicidal, or directly threatening and/or attacking others.

How Involuntary Commitment Works

There are three types of civil commitments:

- *An emergency hospitalization for psychiatric evaluation.* This commonly lasts for a period up to seventy-two hours.
- *A civil commitment as an inpatient.* This is a process whereby a judge orders a person who has symptoms of mental illness to stay for a longer period than the emergency detention period, because they meet the state's legal criteria for a longer commitment. The standards for this commitment vary from state to state, with a main criterion in California, for example, being that the person poses a real and present danger to others.
- *A civil commitment as an outpatient.* Here, a judge orders a person with symptoms of mental illness to participate in a mandatory mental health treatment plan while living in the community. While 44 states permit outpatient commitment, the standards vary from state to state.[1]
    i)

Emergency Commitments

This is the kind of mental health evaluation most widely known, since it involves immediately bringing the behavior of those who appears mentally disturbed to the attention of mental health professionals for treatment and protection for themselves or for others. A common standard that invokes this decision is *when those affected are seen as a danger to themselves or others.*

With the approval of trained mental health professionals or physicians, the police, paramedics, or clinicians can require a person to undergo seventy-two hours of observation in a mental institution by trained psychologists or psychiatrists. These professionals are then given the authority to determine if the person is sane if the crisis that led to their commitment has passed; or if additional assessments are necessary under the danger to self or others standard.

The detention period is designed to provide mental health staff with ample opportunity to determine if the person can be released or requires further treatment. Commonly, such persons are detained from a minimum of up to 48 hours (Georgia) to a maximum of up to 96 hours (Missouri).[2]

Inpatient Civil Commitments

The inpatient civil commitment starts with a petition that a family member, neighbor, or others in the community can file if they believe someone has been acting abnormally and may potentially be insane. The petition leads to a court review and court-ordered hospitalization. The judge makes a decision based on the circumstances described in the petition and any subsequent hearings.

The patient can be released after the initial observation period in the mental hospital. Or, after being committed, the patient can voluntarily extend a stay in a mental hospital if he/she feels more assistance may be necessary.

Outpatient Civil Commitments

Often, a judge uses the same standards as they would use in an inpatient civil commitment to determine a patient should be placed in outpatient care rather than committed in a hospital. But an important difference is that anyone can file such a petition in some states, while in others only certain people can initiate a claim in others.

Common Abuses with Involuntary Commitments

There is absolutely a need for involuntary commitment and for the process to go swiftly when necessary. Lawyer Creigh Deeds was unable to get an emergency commitment for his son Gus recently; consequently, Gus stabbed him and then killed himself.[3] However, one must balance the need for swift processing of involuntary commitments against possible abuse of the process. Abuses can occur in the mental health commitment process, and in a variety of ways. For example, Carol and I discovered all too well that there are insufficient protections in place for a perfectly sane person in countering a claim of insanity by a vindictive individual. Let's look at each kind of commitment, and see what is likely or possible to go wrong.

Abuse of Emergency Commitments

The danger for abuse with the emergency medical evaluation is that trained staffers at an institution are unlikely to turn down the police, paramedics, or a clinician when they bring them a potential patient. Although the police are often justified in bringing in a patient they observe engaging in abnormal and/or potentially dangerous behavior, the police usually do so in response to the complaint of an ordinary citizen. That means in many cases, the police are more afraid of what might happen if they do *not* bring in such an individual — even if they are not in possession of any real facts about the situation at hand. What if the initial report is based on an individual who is angry at, or does not like, the person in question? *Vengeance* or *dislike* can easily trigger the beginning of an emergency commitment process.

Abuses of Inpatient and Outpatient Commitments

Abuse of inpatient commitments can occur in several unique ways. Unlike with emergency commitments, in inpatient and outpatient commitments *a judge* responds to a petition with the decision to commit where the decision and commitment period at the discretion of the individual judge. This is vastly different from emergency commitments, where *the law* limits the length of time for evaluation.

Secondly, abuses can occur during the petition process itself for both inpatient and outpatient commitments. Abuse is present if those petitioning for another's involuntary commitment are mistaken in their judgment of certain behaviors as being indications that the individual requires treatment. And as mentioned, some persons may angrily or vindictively use the involuntary committal process to subject people they do not like or want to hurt to observation and treatment by claiming they are mentally disturbed when they are not.

The most serious problem results in those states where there are loose standards about who can file a petition with the courts without any checks by an unbiased mental health professional to ensure that the person about whom the petition is filed meets the criteria for mental illness. In states where there are few checks in place, it is quite easy for someone with a grudge to claim someone they do not like is mentally ill. The burden of proof is then on the person who has been filed against to show they are not mentally ill. Fortunately, some states, such as California and Georgia, require certain types of mental health professionals to approve the petition by attesting that the person may be mentally ill. However, few states have these built-in protections.

The standard for involuntary commitment does not — and should not — include situations where a person is simply anxious, abrasive, argumentative, annoying, or otherwise rubs people the wrong way. If one person dislikes another or considers their behavior offensive, it is not sufficient grounds to claim someone possesses a severe mental illness. In addition, it is not grounds for committing that person to a mental institution, as was the case when our neighbor built up his charges. It is worrisome to imagine how easily family members could abuse this process to gain control or executorship of an estate.

It was disturbing for both Carol and me to see how easy it was in our state to submit a petition, persuade a judge to agree, and then obtain a commitment order with little penalty offered even if the evidence is later uncovered as false. The individual who files the complaint could always say they did not realize there was anything wrong with the evidence — and in most cases, doing so would mean they would escape any penalty. In Carol's case, there was no opportunity to seek any redress from the system or penalty against our neighbor as both police and prosecutor believed the story without seriously investigating to determine if the claims were true. The prosecutor at Carol's initial commitment hearing played by the rules, but the problem was she had obtained testimony from witnesses who made claims that were misleading or worse.

Moreover, if the defendant's attorney is not adequately prepared to challenge the judge's rulings or counter the testimony, it can result in an involuntary commitment. In our case, Carol did not have "*effective* assistance of counsel," and although she had a right to present evidence on her own behalf, she did not do so because of our attorney's poor advice. She exercised her right to remain silent at our attorney's insistence — and ultimately at great cost to herself. A biased, one-sided picture was all that was presented in court, with our side failing to present countering evidence that 1) Carol was of perfectly sound mind, and 2) the boy that made the initial claim was lying. In hindsight, it seems quite simple as to what we should have done; at the time, it was not.

Other abuses can occur state by state. For example, certain states allow long extensions of the original involuntary commitment if recommended by the mental health facility treating the person. Then, once the patient is subjected to this extended involuntary commitment, the facility is allowed to use both short-acting and long-acting medications on the patient for treatment purposes. Even electro-convulsive therapy might be used if the treatment staff provides clear and convincing proof that such treatment is necessary to the probate court. (The proposed treatment would be included in a treatment plan that is submitted to the court for approval at the hearing held for the extended stay, which then becomes part of the court order for the involuntary admission.) Thus, involuntarily committed persons can find themselves trapped within the system for long and harrowing periods.

While there are provisions for hearings, continuances to obtain evidence and perform investigations, and appeals, the defendant's costs of fighting a system with its treatment plans, mental health professionals, judges, and witnesses is daunting. It is truly difficult for a person who does not believe they are appropriately committed to fight the system. In our case, if Carol did not agree with the treatment provided by the hospital and if she tried to fight the judge's order, she could easily have ended up in an even more Kafka-like nightmare from which any attempt to escape would only be seen as evidence of requiring further treatment — something she did not need in the first place.

What about if an official, physician, or other person should make any mistakes in processing or treating the patient? Unfortunately, for the patient, as long as such involved persons are acting in good faith, there is no recourse. Several states' codes clearly state no physician can be held libel for their actions unless it can be proved they are acting from bad faith, malice or gross negligence.

Uncovering the Policies and Procedures in Your State

Since the mental health laws for involuntary commitment clearly vary somewhat from state to state, here are two key sources so you can find the specifics for your state:

- *The state-by-state guide from the Treatment Advocacy Center for assisting and initiating treatment.* This guide includes the inpatient, outpatient, and emergency hospitalization standards that list the criteria for each type of admission by state and the state code for that requirement.[1]

- The website *JustisUSLaw.com* posts the laws for each individual state. You also can find the codes for your state by putting *law.justa.com/codes/nameofstate* in a search engine. You then find your state's most recent codes, then look for the particular category, such as health and safety codes, and then look for the mental health category. You can also put the term "commitment" and "treatment" and the name of your state in Google, and find the most recent codes available for your state.

HOW TO DO IT BETTER

The following suggestions could improve the mental health involuntary commitment process, and while some states already employ these suggestions, too many states do not:

- *If an individual meets the requirements for filing a petition, then the individuals with the power to approve that petition should include at least one of the following in each category.* The one exception might be in the case of a habitual offender, who has previously been committed two or more times.

Required Legal Approvals :	Required Medical Approvals: (in all types of involuntary commitments from one of the following individuals)
A. Judge (required for all Inpatient and Outpatient Commitments) B. B) Peace or Police Officer (in place of judge for Emergency Commitments only)	A. Psychiatrist or psychologist B. Therapist or Counselor C. Marriage/Family Therapist D. Clinical Social Worker E. Mental Health Emergency Worker F. Health Professional G. Physician

- *Some minimal national standards should be set for determining what allows for an involuntary commitment due to mental illness.*

This would help to avoid the problem where a person could be subjected to an involuntary commitment in one state for mental illness, but not in another state.

- *All states should follow the same list of clear and specific qualities to indicate when someone seems to have a severe mental disturbance and is a danger to themselves and others* (along with tangible behavioral indicators that a person is not to be considered mentally disturbed or dangerous to themselves or others). These might be developed on a national basis by combining the main points made by the standards currently used in different states.

- *Once a petition is filed, the person against whom it is filed should be able to request an outpatient evaluation by a neutral third-party mental health professional prior to making any court appearance.* In the event that this neutral professional deems the petition unfounded, then a judge might decide to review the petition and potentially dismiss it.

- *The person against whom a petition is filed should have the ability to have the initial claim reduced to a lower level of commitment at the time of a hearing.* For example, the person might argue for an outpatient commitment instead of an inpatient commitment. Or, instead of an outpatient commitment, the person might argue for a reduced period of supervision or a stay on the order.

- *A mental health professional should make the determination of any further stay or extension for an individual* — although the individual in question should have a right to dispute that evaluation by filing for a second opinion, as well as a hearing by a judge.

- *There should be national or state requirements for the maximum length of time a person can be involuntarily committed to a mental institution (depending on the type of commitment sought), unless there is a finding by a judge with input from a mental health professional that more time is needed for an evaluation or treatment.* The emergency commitment and inpatient commitment both should be for a maximum of seventy-two hours; the commitment for the outpatient treatment should be a maximum of five days.

- *There should be specific penalties for someone who has filed a frivolous or vindictive petition that is proven to have been be filed without just cause.* In the event an individual feels another person has unreasonably filed a petition against them, then a judge could render judgment based on the usual reasonable belief standard used in other civil cases that is based on a preponderance of the evidence. However, as long as the person who filed the petition has a reasonable belief that the person against whom the petition is filed is mentally ill, then that should eliminate any penalties even if the person turns out to be wrong. But more severe penalties should come into play when an individual uses their position as a mental health professional to intentionally misuse the system against another individual. That person's professional licenses should be revoked, in addition to other penalties, including possible jail time. State licensing boards should be granted the authority to review and act upon any such complaints.

CHAPTER 12: PROSECUTORIAL MISCONDUCT

Prosecutors wield extraordinary power, but just as easily as they can put true criminals behind bars, they can destroy the lives of innocent defendants. Prosecutors are expected to seek truth and justice, but they are also saddled with tremendous pressure from supervisors to aggressively pursue convictions or score "winning" plea bargains. Often, the push to gain convictions — and the praise that follows — can overcome the prosecutorial directive to seek what is true and just. So prosecutors selectively choose which cases to prosecute and how — with limited checks on their conduct.

Since 1997, there have been 201 criminal cases where federal judges determined that select U.S. Department of Justice prosecutors violated laws or ethics rules. Forty-seven of these defendants were exonerated later, with only one federal prosecutor being barred (temporarily) from practicing law for misconduct in the last twelve years.[1] Although more than 700 prosecutors in California committed prosecutorial misconduct between 1997 and 2009 (according to state, federal, and appellate court opinions), a Santa Clara University School of Law study noted that the authorities failed to either report or even discipline these prosecutors. The California State Bar disciplined only six of the prosecutors involved.[2]

In a series of lengthy article on prosecutorial misconduct, journalists Ken Armstrong and Maurice Possley of the *Chicago Tribune* reported, "With impunity, prosecutors across the country have violated their oaths and the law, committing the worst kinds of deception in the most serious of cases... They do it to win. They do it because they won't get punished."[3]

What kind of deception were these prosecutors engaged in? As also pointed out by Armstrong and Possley back in 1999:

- Since a 1963 U.S. Supreme Court ruling designed to curb misconduct by prosecutors, *at least 381 defendants nationally have had a homicide conviction thrown out because prosecutors concealed evidence suggesting innocence or presented evidence they knew to be false.* [emphasis mine]... And that number represents only a fraction of how often such cheating occurs."[3]

- This small number is, in part, because much violation of the act is unreported, since most convicts are impoverished and can't afford representation to adequately fight back against a prosecutor intent on a conviction.[3]

- The U.S. Supreme Court has declared such misconduct by prosecutors to be so reprehensible that it warrants criminal charges and disbarment. But not one of those prosecutors was convicted of a crime. Not one was barred from practicing law. Instead, many saw their careers advance, later to become judges or district attorneys. [3]

There is no indication the situation has ameliorated since that time, with many of the now-publicized cases of prosecutorial misconduct involving convictions supported by incorrectly used DNA evidence. Because of this behavior, more than 250 defendants who were convicted of crimes they did not commit have been exonerated — a revelation exposed only as a result of appeals. Barry Scheck of the Innocence Project notes that only a small number of prosecutors have been sanctioned, even when acts of misconduct have led to cases being overturned:

> *"Our system rarely disciplines, much less brings criminal charges against prosecutors who have engaged in acts of intentional misconduct. Far too often, prosecutors, who wield enormous power over our lives, aren't investigated at all, even for intentional misconduct that has led to a wrongful conviction, much less 'harmless' intentional misconduct in cases in which the defendant was guilty."[4]*

So in what kinds of misbehavior are criminal prosecutors engaged?

Major Types of Prosecutorial Misconduct

Playing Politics with Evidence

One of the most common major types of prosecutorial misconduct is not providing the defense team with all the evidence the prosecution has gathered, in particular evidence that is *exculpatory* (favorable to the defendant). While prosecutors are constitutionally obligated to share exculpatory and other evidence favorable to the defendant with the defense, they are essentially immune from prosecution themselves, and so often ignore this obligation, either intentionally or through negligence.

An example is a prosecutor who knows a witness has recanted his or her statement against the defendant; that results of an investigation or crime lab test have undercut their theory of the case; or that the evidence points to the non-existence of a crime (such as when a victim or witness is lying, or when there is evidence the crime actually resulted from an accident) — and yet the prosecutor chooses not to use this evidence, show it to the defense, and/or close their pursuit of the case.

Not only may a prosecutor downplay or ignore exculpatory evidence — but there are also instances where a prosecutor may actively hide or destroy such evidence, or fabricate other evidence to win their case. These serious breaches of the public trust make a mockery of our justice system, and can lead to wrongful convictions or actions against a defendant.

One high-profile case where the prosecutors concealed evidence to win a case against a high-profile defendant is that of Senator Ted Stevens, a Republican seeking re-election in Alaska. The case revolved around a charge that Stevens had failed to report more than $250,000 in illegal gifts and home renovations received between May 1999 and August 2007. The defendant insisted that he had intended to pay for all of the work performed on his house.

The jury found Stevens guilty of seven felony counts of failing to disclose the renovations and other gifts. A few days after this verdict, Stevens, the longest-serving Republican Senator in history, narrowly lost his re-election bid.

Less than a year later, a U.S. District Judge threw out the case at the request of the Justice Department, which found that exculpatory evidence had been withheld at the trial. The judge, Emmet G. Sullivan, took the unprecedented step to appoint a court-appointed special counsel, Henry F. Schuelke III, to investigate the six prosecutors who had handled Stevens's investigation and trial. After a two-year investigation of more than 128,000 pages of documents, Schuelke concluded, "Significant evidence was not disclosed to the defense and critical mistakes were made throughout the course of the trial that denied Senator Stevens a fair opportunity to defend himself." In short, the prosecutors withheld all sorts of materials that would have supported Senator Stevens's contention that he had intended to pay. Thus, the prosecutors won their conviction through intentionally withholding and concealing evidence.

While Schuelke stated the prosecutors' actions were "...broadly illegal," he also said he could not bring criminal contempt charges against the two prosecutors who had "intentionally withheld exculpatory information *because the judge had not specifically issued an order telling them to turn over such evidence*"[5] [emphasis mine]. The prosecutors in question escaped with little punishment aside from an admonition for their bad behavior.

Ignoring Evidence of a Witness's Lies, and/or Leaking Inflammatory and Prejudicial Information

Misconduct occurs when a prosecutor improperly relies on the testimony of unreliable witnesses to make their case, or on those with an axe to grind. Or, a prosecutor can choose to rely on the use of "snitches" who are in jail or facing criminal charges, and who are lying in order to reduce their sentence or evade the charges against them entirely.

A prosecutor also might deliberately reveal to the press prejudicial and inflammatory information to support their personal belief a defendant is guilty in advance of a trial. This is exactly what a prosecutor did in the notorious Duke University lacrosse team case in which three players were falsely accused of rape. The prosecutorial misconduct in this case was so great that the prosecutor was criminally charged for his crime, disbarred, fined, convicted, and served a short jail sentence.

The case began in March 2006, after the Duke men's lacrosse team held a party at which they had arranged for two strippers to appear. There were some arguments in the house between the men and the strippers during their performance, and shortly before one a.m., the strippers, Crystal Mangum and Kim Roberts entered a car and drove off. After the two women got into an argument in a parking lot, police took Mangum, an African-American, to the Durham Access Center, a mental-health and substance abuse facility for involuntary commitment. While Mangum was being admitted, she claimed she had been raped at the house, and was transferred to the Duke University Medical Center for tests. She received treatment there for some genital injuries, but it was unclear that her injuries were consistent with rape.

Although Mangum's story kept changing and vast evidence existed to the contrary, prosecutor Mike Nifong proceeded as if this was a slam-dunk case of rape. He did everything in his power to prove it regardless of what the evidence showed, and he sought to make his case in the court of public opinion through media leaks as well as in court. The prosecution ordered the members of the team to provide DNA samples and had them analyzed at two different labs, but none had a DNA match, although the tests showed DNA from multiple males inside Mangum and on her underwear. Undeterred, Nifong continued with the case.

The results of Nifong's charges of first-degree forcible rape, first-degree sexual offense, and kidnapping along with other information he released to the media were devastating to the three defendants charged as well as the school. What made the story even more explosive was that the prosecution charged the alleged assault was a hate crime.

After Nifong framed the issue as one of race hatred by rich white fraternity boys against minority women, there were threats of gang violence against the general Duke student population. The press stirred up emotions too by vilifying the lacrosse team players for their attack on the two women. In effect, Nifong was able to stir up public opinion to ensure the three men charged with the crime would be considered guilty even before the case went to trial.

Unknown to the public at that time, Mangum had a long history of mental problems and had been previously diagnosed with bipolar disorder. Mangum had also made a similar rape claim ten years before in 1995 (although she repeatedly changed her story, and had never pursued it). In the Duke case, she also changed her descriptions of the three men who raped her to the police. Moreover, the testimony of the second stripper, Kim Roberts undermined her claim, since she stated Mangum was not raped.

Despite the obvious flaws in the case, Nifong continued to pursue it for another six months. Eventually, Nifong withdrew himself from the case and turned it over to North Carolina Attorney General Roy Cooper. After further investigating the case, Cooper dismissed all charges against the three players and further declared that they were innocent. As Cooper stated in making his announcement: "We have no credible evidence that an attack occurred." [7]

Cooper then pursued charges against Nifong, declaring him a "rogue prosecutor." A three-member disciplinary panel found him guilty of numerous acts of prosecutorial misconduct, among them: "fraud, dishonesty, deceit or misrepresentation... making false statements of material fact before a judge... making false statements of material fact before bar investigations, and... lying about withholding exculpatory DNA evidence." In passing judgment, Superior Court Judge W. Osmond Smith III found Nifong in contempt, because he had lied to the court during a hearing the previous September about whether all DNA evidence had been provided to defense attorneys. [8]

Nifong was disbarred and convicted of criminal contempt for knowingly making false statements during criminal proceedings. His sentence? A day in jail. Although his single day in jail might seem a slap on the wrist given all the havoc Nifong caused, it was one of the few times a prosecutor received *any* punishment for misconduct. At the time, Nifong's motivation to use the case to run for office was well-concealed, although subsequently a *New York Times* article later noted this motivation in describing how the case came to be viewed by many: "as a morality play of justice run off the rails by political correctness (i.e.: because of the many people who were all too ready to see this as a hate crime against a black woman) and the political ambitions of Mr. Nifong."[7]

So if politics was Nifong's motivation, are there other reasons for prosecutorial misconduct? *Why is prosecutorial misconduct so rampant?*

Motivations for Prosecutorial Misconduct

Sometimes, prosecutors in criminal cases engage in misconduct in order to obtain bogus evidence to convict the defendants, all because they believe the defendants really *are* guilty. To this end, prosecutors may intentionally plant, lose, or tamper with evidence, improperly coerce or reward witnesses, and/or suppress exculpatory evidence or information.[9]

Other times, outside pressures on what cases to charge can easily sway prosecutors to try one case over another. Prosecutors are liable to succumb to this influence as they have wide discretion in choosing what cases they want to prosecute.

Another common reason (mentioned earlier) is that prosecutors are often faced with immense pressure from supervisors to win cases. As a result, despite their affirmative duty to turn over all evidence to the defendant, many do not because they feel pressure to obtain a guilty verdict at all costs.[10] And—although this may not always literally qualify as 'misconduct' — in a misguided effort to quickly convict and punish a suspect, prosecutors also often focus on the wrong individual, ignoring other facts or evidence in the process.

And, since there are weak sanctions for any misbehavior, prosecutors are largely free to do what they want without fear of any reprisal.[11]

HOW TO DO IT BETTER

With the power of prosecutors nearly absolute, and some innocent defendants able to do little because they are seriously "outgunned" by the power of the prosecutors, it is important for us to change things. Part of our reason for telling Carol's story (apart from setting the record straight) is to showcase some of the glaring problems in the criminal justice system in the hopes to motivate enough people and government officials to seek change.

- Perhaps one incentive to generate better prosecutorial conduct might be *finding a way to increase the pay for prosecutors since they are poorly paid compared to most lawyers.* With more pay, they may be more willing to focus on the merits of the case, and less likely to view it as a mere stepping-stone to a higher-level position with more income. When one values something and plans to hold onto it for a long period, one treats it better, and with respect.

- Secondly, just as lawyers need to go back every year or two for refresher classes on ethics, *prosecutors should be required to attend a similar program each year to remind them of their sworn duty to pursue the truth.*

- Third: we must address *the real need for qualified (as opposed to absolute) immunity for prosecutors.* For more on this suggestion, see Chapter 18.

Doing It Better

In 2006, Texas's Dallas County elected a new District Attorney, Craig Watkins. The first-ever African-American elected district attorney in Texas history, Watkins has taken a very different stance toward criminal prosecutions than his predecessors.

To deal with the fact that Dallas had more DNA exonerations than any other county in the U.S., Watkins partnered with the Innocence Project of Texas to review hundreds of requests for DNA testing. This gained national attention. But he also made other fundamental local changes that affected far more cases. Watkins "shook up" his office. After framing and placing on workroom walls an article of the "Texas Code of Criminal procedure with only one sentence highlighted — '**It shall be the duty of all prosecuting attorneys, including any special prosecutors, not to convict but to see that justice is done'** — he went about seeing that some top-level prosecutors were fired. Others left.[12]

Another favorite Watkins quotation is, "Our success is not going to be based on the number of folks we send to prison or death row. That's just evidence of the failure of the criminal justice system."[12]

Author Mark Donald says that Watkins:

"...delicately balances the traditional role of a prosecutor as community enforcer against the more holistic approach of a prosecutor as community problem-solver. That balance has Watkins one day issuing a press release announcing he will seek the death penalty against an alleged cop killer and the next day rewarding a prosecutor for initiating a Big Brother program that pairs DA staffers with the children of inmates. It has him one day touting his new absconder unit, which will hunt down the most violent probation violators before they can victimize again, and another day selling his ideas about a community court system so neighborhood elders can punish defendants in such a way that victims will be made whole again." [12]

Those voters re-elected Watkins in 2010.

Kudos to Watkins—and kudos to those Texas citizens.

CHAPTER 13: POOR JUDICIAL BEHAVIOR

Judges wield an enormous amount of power in the judicial system. Although judges do not receive the kind of public attention that prosecutors receive when they behave badly, their misbehavior can prove equally devastating.

The behavioral standards to which judges are supposed to adhere are spelled out in the *Code of Judicial Conduct*, which is designed to guide judges and candidates for judicial office on how to act, as well as provide a structure against which their conduct can be measured in the case of any complaints. These standards are guided by two central principles: First, judges should treat their judicial office as a "public trust." Second, they should "strive to maintain and enhance the public's confidence in our legal system" — which means conduct themselves with the proper decorum both in and outside the courtroom.[1]

Judges cannot allow family, social, or political relationships to influence how they decide a case. Nor should they hear or preside over a case if there exists a conflict of interest, which can include a personal relationship with one party or a personal interest in the outcome of the case. Judges must remain impartial. Always. Should that impartiality be in doubt, they should disqualify themselves.

Judges also must avoid any appearance of impropriety, and refrain from giving or receiving any sort of gift, loan, or other favor from a lawyer, witness, or any party to the case. To attest to their independence of influence, judges are required to file financial disclosure statements with the court and state ethics commission.[1]

Yet despite the existence of some checks on their conduct, judges can and do act in ways that fall short of the standard for the office they hold.

Abuses of Judicial Power

Improper Courtroom Behavior

The proper calm, impartial, and respectful behavior normally characteristic of judges has been very distorted by the presentation of court cases on TV. These courtroom shows feature caricatures of judges like Judge Judy[2], a former judge who insults and embarrasses whomever she thinks has done wrong. In effect, she treats persons in her courtroom as if they are naughty children who need to be slapped. Such judicial behavior might make for entertaining TV — but undermines the proper courtroom decorum the public should actually expect of a judge.

There are many way in which today's judges can fall short in the courtroom. Some failings are:

Habitual intemperance, such as having an angry, sarcastic tone in making comments in the court; or insulting, ridiculing, or disparaging counsel, the parties, jurors, or witnesses in a case. Judges should display patience, dignity, and courtesy.[3]

Conduct unbecoming a judicial officer, which can occur on the bench or in a judge's personal life. Such behavior can bring a judicial office into disrepute, such as turning one's court into a kind of circus à la Judge Judy.

Conduct prejudicial to the administration of justice, such as demonstrating a clear preference for one side or the other (usually the prosecutor), and ruling with a bias toward that side.

Showing Bias

Many judges exhibit a bias in favor of the prosecution. Prosecutors represent the state and the community — which are aligned against the defendant — and judges generally identify with the establishment. Thus, when any defendant goes to court, it is like approaching a dealer with a stacked deck that favors the house.

Judges have numerous options that make it "amazingly easy…to fix the outcome of a trial."[4] These methods include:

- Manipulating the jury selection process;
- Deciding which witnesses can testify and what testimony they are allowed to provide;
- Determining the physical and documentary items that can be introduced as evidence;
- Deciding which objections are sustained or overruled;
- Conveying to the jurors how the judge perceives the defendant and defense lawyer by the judge's tone of voice and body language;
- Providing the instructions to the jury as to the law, and how to apply it to those facts which the judge permits the jurors to see and hear;[4]
- Improperly sharing privileged information with prosecutors outside the courtroom, either in chambers or during social interactions.

If and when a judge behaves in the ways described above, the defendant is being "judicially sandbagged… the judge's opinions of a person's guilt or innocence can be the primary determinate of a trial's outcome, and not whether the person is actually innocent or guilty."[4] Given these contributions of judicial bias to the courtroom, prosecutors end up more likely to win their cases. To cite Sherrer:

> *Playing an important role in a judge's subtle manipulation of the proceedings in his/her courtroom is the judge's use of mind control techniques on jurors – the same techniques…used by law enforcement interrogators to extract false confessions from innocent men and women…The use of these insidious techniques…is a significant contributor to wrongful convictions…this power is often used to the detriment of innocent men and women, because a judge can use all the methods and nuances of his craft to steer trial in the direction of concluding in the way he or she has pre-determined it should end.* [4]

There have been numerous cases after a trial where the jurors, once free of any judicial pressure, have noted that they arrived at a guilty verdict based on what the judge in effect "told" them to do via tone and/or body language.

The Power to Do Harm

Judges hold a tremendous power to do harm to defendants. For example, from their protected perch, a judge can order the police or sheriff to physically seize and drag a defendant to jail if they decline to comply with a judicial command. By the same token, a judge can have someone thrown into jail for contempt of court if the individual does not show proper respect.

Yet the aura of civility and decorum that may be present in the courtroom in turn can mask the true "horror" judges can inflict on innocent defendants by their pronouncements. Lives can be completely turned around and decimated by the flick of a pen. Faced with the prospect of going to trial with Judge Self as the judge, Carol had good reason to be afraid: She had already been traumatized by the judge's attitude and scolding. In turn, she was afraid to face a jury that might be influenced by him to render a guilty verdict. Judge Self appeared eager to harshly penalize her, all because she was unwilling to have her case decided by him alone, without a jury.

The mere fear of the judge's power to influence a jury's decision might lead a defendant to accept a damaging and unfair plea. A jury might be influenced by a judge's negative attitude toward the defendant, or by a judge's unfriendly or unsympathetic reaction to defense witnesses and defense attorney: "Judges are able to communicate their biases to jurors not only by non-verbal facial expressions or gestures, but also by friendly or hostile questioning of prosecution or defense witnesses."[5]

Pressuring Defendants to Take Plea Bargains and Make Guilty Pleas

The vast majority of criminal cases are resolved by *plea bargains* — without which the criminal justice system could not function, as the courts would be overwhelmed by cases. Normally, these bargains are resolved by negotiations between the prosecutor and defense attorney. The more judges become involved, the more this can be prejudicial against the defendant.[5]

A key reason judges do get involved is administrative: by encouraging defendants to enter guilty pleas, they can move the court calendar forward. Their involvement can put unwarranted pressure on the defendant, whose own lawyer with a busy caseload and prosecutor eager to rack up another win might already be encouraging the defendant to plead. Such a plea may not be in the defendant's best interest though, so if the judge applies additional pressure on the defendant, it undermines the judge's impartiality in the case.

Carol took a plea that required us to move out of the neighborhood, all because she was afraid of a potential sixteen-year jail term, even though that term would have been unwarranted. And Judge Self was involved in her accepting a plea bargain. As the newspaper reported, "[Judge] Self said he'd allow Clark-Brakke out of jail only if she [Carol] enrolled in an inpatient treatment program or if the defense and prosecutors work out some sort of arrangement 'to keep her out of her Sunken Valley neighborhood.' Further showing his bias, Self added, "I don't want her back on Pearly Lane again — even to pack her bags."

When the defense attorney and prosecutor are unable to obtain a plea bargain, the judge may put pressure on the defendant to enter a guilty plea. Commonly, the judge views the defendant as the "recalcitrant party" and so applies this pressure to "get rid of" the case.[5] To this end, this pressure can involve telling a defendant that if they do not enter a guilty plea *that day*, the judge will not impose a favorable sentence in the future. For instance, the judge might say something like this to a defendant: "This is a one-time offer;" "This offer is for today only;" or "I'll make sure you get sentenced to the max if you don't plead guilty now." Or, a judge might advise the defense counsel thusly: "I strongly suggest that you ask your client to consider a plea, because if the jury returns a verdict of guilty, I might be disposed to impose a substantial prison sentence."[5]

In one Supreme Court of New York case, the judge told a defendant if he refused the offered plea and went to trial, he would make sure the defendant would be "sentenced to the maximum time of incarceration permitted by law."[5] In a particularly horrifying New York case, the presiding judge was adamant that the teenage male defendant accept a plea, although the defendant kept refusing to plead guilty. In his last words to the judge, the defendant said, "I'm nineteen-years-old, Your Honor. That is terrible. That's terrible." The defendant then turned to face his weeping mother and said, "Mom, I can't do it," before jumping out the sixteenth-floor-courtroom window to his death. *This defendant committed suicide rather than face the prospect of a conviction.* Because of the suicide, the case was featured in the media, but the judge's wrongful coercive tactics got little mention.[5]

It is also wrong when a judge uses an excessively high bail amount to persuade a defendant to take a plea. The main purpose of bail is to make sure the defendant shows up in court. However, judges may go along with a prosecutor's vindictive bail request, or set very high bail in misdemeanor cases all on their own, just so the defendant will not be able to make bail. Typically, such judges then tell the defendant that if they plead guilty, they can receive a sentence of "time served" or no jail time.[5] Such judges routinely fail to advise the defendant of all the repercussions to pleading guilty to a crime that might have led the defendant to decline a plea deal. For example, a guilty plea may greatly increase the likelihood there could be civil damages awarded, as well as the loss of other rights, such as forgoing the right to an appeal.[5] We will cover more on rights lost in Chapter 16 and Chapter 17. Yet given the threat of going to prison, even innocent defendants frequently enter pleas. Consequently, they are branded as convicted criminals and they must wear that badge of shame for the rest of their lives.

Motivations for Judicial Bias

Political and Prosecutorial Bias

Whether elected or appointed, a judge is beholden to the community and the power brokers that represent the community. In the event the judge is elected, it is common for their nomination to arise from such power brokers — who are apt to choose whomever best represents their interests. And, as most community members know little more about the judicial candidates beyond what is revealed in their campaign pictures and a short caption or bio, they can be easily swayed in support of a judicial candidate.

- he idea that the voters themselves select their judges is something of a farce. The real electors are a few political leaders who do the nominating... Political leaders nominate practically anybody whom they choose... the voters, as a whole, know little more about the candidates than what their campaign pictures may reveal.

- he fact that most state judges are elected in near anonymity by voters who do not know who they are, compounds the effects of the corrupting nature of the campaign process that ensures their lack of impartiality. Thus, the circumstances under which state judges are elected or nominated and confirmed creates a situation in which the people who become state and federal judges serve their own interests and those whom they are responsible to, and not those of society at large.[4]

With this in mind, judges are more apt to seek to serve the interests of themselves and their supporters before that of than the general community. Sherrer writes that when it comes to politics:

- Contrary to their carefully cultivated public image of being independent and above the frays of everyday life, judges are influenced and even controlled by powerful and largely-hidden political, financial, personal and ideological considerations...[4]
- This political influence on judges operates on all levels of the system — from federal to state judgeships, whether elected, appointed, or running unopposed.

- The political nature of judges that affects their conduct and rulings is an extension of the fact that there is not a single judge in the United States, whether nominated or elected, whether state or federal, that is not a product of the political process as surely as every other political official...[4]

Similarly, judges tend to display prosecutorial bias, due to both politics and the fact that the sentiments of the surrounding community are usually aligned with the goal of the prosecutor to win. As Sherrer puts it, judges "have a strong tendency to go with the flow of outside pressures," especially when there is a "media and politically inspired hysteria" campaign to get tough.[4]

This bias toward the prosecution is even more pronounced when a judge has some sort of a personal connection with the prosecutor, such as that which existed between Judge Self and our prosecutor (in our case, prosecutor Root had clerked in the judge's office).

Personal Bias and Discrimination

The ideal is that judges are not supposed to exhibit a bias or prejudice against any class of people — including prejudice based on race, sex, religion, national origin, disability, age, sexual orientation, or socioeconomic status. The reality is that as people, judges are not exempt from engaging in their own form of personal discrimination or judgment. In our case, the judge, prosecutor, and most witnesses were considerably younger and more Scots-Irish-Anglo than Carol or her lawyer.

Judicial history has shown judges sometimes make statements during trials that are biased. In one such case, the presiding judge sentenced the female teacher convicted of a sexual relationship with a thirteen-year-old boy to probation *instead of the three-year jail sentence to which she had already agreed!* He went on to downplay any harm this woman had caused her victim, stating in part: "Maybe it was a way of (the victim) to, once this did happen, to satisfy his sexual needs. At 13, if you think back, people mature at different ages." The judge then went on to cite newspaper and TV reports in which nine-year-olds were reported to have had sex.[6]

Ultimately, the New Jersey Supreme Court committee found that this judge's statements expressed stereotypical views about the sexual nature of young boys, and noted this judge's views were "...problematic and suspect... fundamentally inconsistent with the meaning and policy of the law that criminalizes the sexual activities between an adult and a minor, boy or girl." Most importantly, the committee complained that the judge was not only mistaken about the law of sexual assault regarding a minor boy, but his remarks reflected a bias, and showed a lack of impartiality and open-mindedness in applying the law.[6]

For acting in this manner, the New Jersey judge was publicly reprimanded by the Supreme Court of New Jersey, nothing more.

Unaccountability in a Conveyor Belt System

As has been the case with prosecutors (see previous chapter), judges are commonly unaccountable or immune for their actions (i.e. however biased they may be in favor of the prosecution).

And in order that cases might be processed as quickly as possible (lest it be overwhelmed by the sheer numbers of cases that enter it), the system is designed like a conveyor belt, with a prime goal of judges being to "keep the assembly-line of the law enforcement system humming smoothly along," and "The huge numbers of innocent men and women who are thrown on the conveyor belt and crushed as the gears grind away are treated as if they are unknown, faceless, and their sole value as a human being is being used as fuel to keep the 'law enforcement' machine running."[4] The result is a system of unaccountability, with judges protected in numerous ways.

First and most importantly, *judges have an absolute immunity to being sued by anyone for anything they do when acting in their official capacity.* This immunity applies even when a judge is accused of "acting maliciously and corruptly." The rationale for this protection is to enable judges to independently exercise their judicial role without fear of the consequences.[4] As a result, an innocent victim of a judge's intentional and malicious actions cannot sue a judge civilly for the harm they have caused. To quote Sherrer: "There is simply no cost to a judge for presiding over the wrongful conviction of an actually innocent person."[4] About the worst that can happen to biased judges is they do not get reappointed, or are voted out of office and retire on a comfortable pension. Actual removal from the bench is rare.

After an extensive study of judicial misbehavior complaints filed with the judicial conduct commissions in fifty states, lawyer Cynthia Gray, director of the American Judicature Society's Center for Judicial Ethics, noted that 90% of such complaints are dismissed every year.[6] A key reason for this was that it is considered "unfair to sanction a judge for not being infallible while making hundreds of decisions often under pressure."[6]

In the event a judge is subject to some kind of discipline, rarely does this mean that judge will be removed from their position. Rather, they may be reprimanded, censured, or suspended for a time before they return to the bench.

Peers on Judicial Disciplinary Panels

The number of judges that behave poorly in all types of courts — from federal to state courts at various levels — is huge, as is the percentage of judges who get away with misbehavior or abuse. A key reason judges usually escape censure is that any disciplinary or investigative panels are usually composed of judges themselves, and such peers are not likely to pass harsh judgment on their fellows.

For example, although 1,163 complaints were filed against federal judges in a one-year period, only four led to any type of disciplinary action, including one public censure.[7] The results were much the same in state courts. Of 909 judicial complaints in California, for instance, only thirty-four or 3.8% resulted in disciplinary actions, ranging from advisory letters to removal from the bench. Of 1,923 complaints in New York, only 3% led to any discipline, including thirty-three letters of caution and twenty-six formal charges.[7]

Given a lack of judicial punishment except in rare cases, it is no wonder judges feel free to behave badly or unethically. Then, too, judges might find it easier to engage in such poor behavior because their judicial immunity protects them from any civil liability when their actions occur while performing judicial duties. Thus, they can't be held personally accountable.

Limitations on Citizen Complaints

This guideline exempts most judicial conduct from citizen complaints: *A defendant or any other interested party cannot complain about the actual decision itself — even if it was incorrect.* About 90% of all citizen complaints get tossed out on this basis alone.

Citizens can only complain about the judicial process itself, such as if a judge seemed to have a conflict of interest, or was not paying attention and as a result may have missed crucial evidence in a case. Unfortunately, there are only a few ways a defendant can currently seek redress, and many limitations exist here too.

To remedy a verdict, for instance, a person must appeal the ruling. However, while anyone can file an appeal, the appeal is a very complicated process that involves arguing the errors made and drawing on the relevant points of law in a case in front of a judge. It is difficult to find an attorney with a specialty in appellate work — not to mention expensive — and so most defendants of limited means lack the resources to appeal a case.

The only way to remedy bad behavior by judges is to file a complaint against a judge — although even such a complaint won't normally remedy a bad decision.

HOW TO DO IT BETTER

While there is little effective recourse to punish poor judicial behavior, the following points can serve as a starting point for a discussion about what we can do to change the judicial system itself:

- *Judges should be required to disqualify themselves from any cases that involve attorneys who have clerked with them.* Furthermore, a list that shows the names of everyone who has ever clerked for them should be on file with the courts and available for public viewing.
- *Prospective judges should be required to submit to a psychological assessment to determine if they possess the appropriate judicial temperament and skills.*
- *Separate elections of judges should be held for inner cities, suburban areas and rural areas.* This change in the voting system would result in returning the exercise of justice back to local populations, which is important because prosecutors and judges are usually elected at the county level. Today, counties that include major cities have a much higher percentage of suburban voters than in the past. This means suburban voters, for whom crime is usually a minor issue, exercise more power over urban criminal justice than in the past." [8]
- *Judicial campaigns should be funded by public financing to prevent big campaign contributions from special interests, which*

can influence judicial decisions in the future. Public financing for this purpose is already in effect in North Carolina as of this writing.

- *Review boards for judicial misconduct should be composed of lawyers from different districts or civilians, with only a minority representation by other judges.* A review board that adds lawyers and civilians to it can provide a broader cross-section of the community and thus offer a more neutral and objective environment for fairly evaluating a judge's performance.

- *The judicial disciplinary review process should be transparent, so citizens can see what complaints are being handled and how.*

- *Cameras should be permitted in the courtroom, not for release to the public or the media. Release of videos should be restricted to lawyers for the purposes of documenting judicial misbehavior as the basis for filing an appeal.* In order to keep the recordings from the media, the recordings should be made exempt from the Freedom of Information Act.

- *Judge Judy-type television shows, which typically show judges behaving badly, should include an advisory that the show is presented purely as entertainment, and does not portray accurately how judges are supposed to comport themselves in a courtroom.*

CHAPTER 14: THE MEDIA'S ROLE

Today, the media have become complicit in producing unfair treatment, trials, and verdicts for defendants. They sensationalize cases; pick and choose whatever elements of a case make it unusual and "newsworthy;" and otherwise draw what often becomes negative public attention to private citizens. Given the ability of the media to pick up local reports and turn them into compelling national stories, even juicy day-to-day gossip can become a national event.

Cases that involve celebrities or government officials can fare even worse.

Prosecutorial bias is at work in the media, and a key reason is that prosecutors are eager to feed the media information. In contrast, defense lawyers generally want to avoid getting their client in the news as much as possible. Consequently, the media tends to portray defendants as more likely to be guilty than innocent. For example, the media also often repeats statements made about the defendant that have yet to be proven true. Unfortunately, even if these claims later prove erroneous, the damage cannot be undone. While the media seeks to justify its actions in the name of the "public's right to know," it often steps over the line in compromising the defendant's right to a fair trial. Unfortunately, the media generally takes no responsibility for the harm it causes, since after the excitement of the case is over, it is already on to the next "big" story.

In Carol's case, we were turned down twice after approaching a local paper to print a follow-up story on their back pages to present our side of the story. However, when Carol and I examined the system more in general, we found that our suffering was slight compared to that of many persons caught within the snares of today's increasingly unreasonable criminal justice system.

Abuses by the Media

Making a Defendant Look Guilty

Sometimes, the media can turn public opinion against a defendant just by what they report (or fail to report) regarding statements made in public, interviews with the press, or in court. As such, the media can make an innocent defendant appear remarkably guilty by bringing up past behaviors or associations, suggesting a motive, or otherwise framing various past circumstances within a theory that purportedly "proves" a predisposition to commit a crime. While judges generally do not allow such prejudicial examples to be presented in the actual criminal case, it is rare for them to be able to prevent the media from reporting such information outside the courtroom under the guise of "investigative journalism." Unfortunately, the reality then is that potential jurors are exposed to such information, something that, despite their own best efforts, can influence their supposedly neutral analysis of the evidence and testimony in a case. As such, sometimes defense lawyers ask to have a case moved to another location, one that has not reported too much on the story.

The media can also make a defendant seem guilty by playing up their reaction after being charged with a crime. If the reaction seems lighthearted or inappropriate, the media may target that behavior as a sign of guilt — something which can also influence jurors.

One way the media protects itself from being accused of bias against a defendant results from its general claim that it is "just a messenger" and merely reporting on what was already "said by the police or prosecutors." In addition, the media commonly releases information on the TV or Internet with insertions of numerous "alleged" descriptors to suggest that the defendant is only a "possible" suspect who has "allegedly" committed a crime. The media's use of the word "alleged" protects it from libel or slander, either written or spoken. Just listen to the morning or nightly news, and you will hear the word "alleged" used numerous times in a daily report on national or local crime.

Yet nearly invariably, even when the defendant's guilt is qualified by the term "alleged," the public responds with an assumption of the defendant's guilt. "Innocent until proven guilty" becomes "guilty until proven innocent," and it becomes difficult to change people's minds after the fact even if ultimately they are shown a more plausible interpretation of the facts.

Psychological research has shown that once people take a position, they are more receptive to information in the future that confirms the impression they have already formed than to listening to and/or accepting information that contradicts their position. As Chief Justice Thurgood Marshall pointed out, a juror "will listen more with favor to that testimony which confirms than to that which will change his opinion; it is not to be expected that he will weigh evidence or argument as fairly as a man whose judgment is not made up in the case."[1]

Notorious Pre-Trial (and Trial) Publicity

Too much publicity not only attracts viewers and sells newspapers or draws viewers to websites, but it can destroy a defendant's chance to get a fair trial. That is what happened in the notorious Sam Sheppard trial in which the defendant, a doctor, was accused of murdering his wife. In this 1954 case, Sheppard maintained an intruder knocked him unconscious and killed his wife, but the coroner (Gerber) was overheard telling a detective, "It's obvious that the doctor did it," a quote that soon appeared in the media.

The press turned against Sheppard with a fury before he was even charged with anything! Statements and leaks by the prosecution helped add fuel to the media fire, with the *Cleveland Press* quoting Assistant Prosecutor John Mahon as declaring four days after the murder: "In my twenty-three years of criminal investigation, I have never seen such flagrant stalling as in this case by the family." Soon thereafter, a front-page editorial screamed out to law enforcement and the public with the cry, "WHY NO INQUEST? DO IT NOW, DR. GERBER."[2]

The police quickly responded with Sheppard's arrest. By the time the actual trial started, the trial had already become a media circus: "Celebrity journalists flocked to the city for a trial that promised sex, mystery, and intrigue in abundance."[2] Amazingly, even the judge — Judge Edward Blythin — shared his opinion of the ongoing case with a reporter (although the reporter only reported his statements nearly a decade later, after the judge's death). Apparently, the judge told the reporter: "The case is open and shut… he's guilty as hell."

Despite defense motions to move the trial out of the city in which the murder occurred, or at least delay it until publicity about the case died down, the judge refused, so the trial proceeded with a jury already mired in public opinion against Sheppard. Worse, the jury's ability to remain impartial was further compromised when Cleveland newspapers published all the jurors' photos and names. *Given the strong community sentiment against Sheppard, what identified juror would dare buck community opinion and approach the case without bias?*

Not surprisingly, the jury found Sheppard guilty of second-degree murder, and Judge Blythin sentenced Sheppard to life in prison. However, things turned around when a new defense lawyer, F. Lee Bailey, took over the case after the death of Sheppard's first lawyer. In 1963, Bailey filed a petition that claimed, "Prejudicial publicity before and during the 1954 trial violated Sheppard's right to the due process of law."[2] Eventually, the case reached the U.S. Supreme Court, which agreed that the publicity surrounding his trial had prejudiced his "right to trial by an impartial jury." The Court also provided some guidelines to help judges keep the courtroom impartial in the face of publicity from the media. In particular, the Court said a judge should:

- Set rules for in-court conduct by reporters;
- Grant continuances for a later trial;
- Grant a change of venue to keep prospective jurors unbiased;
- Admonish the jury to ignore publicity;
- Sequester the jury to insulate them from publicity; and/or
- Issue protective orders (gag orders) for out of court statements by trial participants.[3]

However, the Court's ruling did not take Sheppard off the hook, because within days prosecutors decided to retry him. This time, the defense prevailed by bringing up blood-spatter evidence that showed the killer was left-handed, whereas Sheppard was right-handed. F. Lee Bailey also showed there was blood on the closet door that came from neither Sheppard nor his wife, and was presumably left by the killer. As a result, the jury acquitted Sheppard.[4]

In Sheppard's case, the media played a critical role in distorting the justice process from the very beginning, and the U.S Supreme Court recognized that the negative publicity had made it impossible for Sheppard to get a fair trial.

It is interesting that in Britain, newspapers, periodicals and broadcasters can only publish or include the following basic information about a case in their reports: the identity of the court and the name of the judge; the names, ages, home addresses and occupations of the accused and witnesses; the offense or offenses charged; the names of the lawyers in the proceeding; any date and place to which the proceedings are adjourned; any arrangements for bail; and whether legal aid was granted to the accused. This approach is designed to keep the reporters from reporting details of the case that may prove inflammatory to the defendant.[5]

Across Multiple Platforms and from Unnamed Sources

As recently shown, the media can turn virtually any case into a highly publicized one—and more so in today's world by virtue of the multiple media platforms now in existence. Nowadays, many mediums, including online e-zines, news aggregators like *Drudge Report*, individual bloggers, social media commentators on Facebook, Twitter, and Google+, and other media on mobile devices are apt to pick up on a story released initially by one outlet. A recent example is an alleged University of Virginia rape case reported by Rolling Stone magazine in 2014 and then picked up by the national media. It caused much turmoil but was soon found to be a false allegation.[6]

At one time, the courtroom operated fairly free of the influence of newspapers since news articles relevant to the case at hand were cut out of the daily paper before it was handed to the jurors. But today, it is difficult to redact anything, given the pervasiveness of the news on multiple media platforms. Many jurors are liable to become aware of and be influenced by information nowadays through simply reading the news of the day on the Internet, or reading through their emails, which can include updates and flashes from various news sources.

Moreover, some jurors, already accustomed to tweeting or blogging about whatever they are doing in their personal lives, may find it easy to slip and make an inappropriate comment about their respective participation in a trial.

Oftentimes too, a reporter will cite an unnamed "source" as the basis for a story, and claim it a "journalist's privilege" to protect the identity of their sources.

Racial Bias

Often, the race of a defendant or victim plays a part in contributing to the public's belief (inflamed by the media) that a defendant is guilty. In the highly publicized Rodney King case, a predominantly white jury exonerated white L.A. police officers who brutally beat King. This outcome provoked a riot.[7]

Racial overtones likewise contributed to the O.J. Simpson case.[8] Based on Simpson's behavior in the SUV "chase" that dragged on for hours on live TV, most whites assumed he had to be guilty. As it dragged on, the case turned into a litmus test of race relations. Whites formed the impression O.J. was guilty, but escaped true justice because of his celebrity status and team of slick, expensive lawyers. By contrast, African-Americans commonly thought O.J. had been railroaded by the system because of his race and marriage to a white woman. Simpson was eventually declared "not guilty" by a predominantly African-Americans jury in a criminal case, but found guilty by a primarily white jury in a subsequent civil case. Later he was sent to prison for his role in robbing a man selling his sports paraphernalia, perhaps as payback for the acquittal in the criminal trial, though the general public was widely convinced of his guilt. And now the mostly tabloid media has been playing up stories of new evidence showing his guilt, a bombshell confession that he did it made to a cellmate, and how Simpson is dying in prison — a kind of new trial and punishment by media over 20 years after the original 1994 trial.

The Trayvon Martin/George Zimmerman case in Florida initially began as a killing by a local neighborhood-watch captain who thought a man he saw in a gated community was acting suspiciously. However, the victim Martin was African-American, while Zimmerman was perceived as white (he is actually part Hispanic). Thus, the killing easily fit into a portrayal of whites who use racial profiling to target African-Americans as criminals. Soon, African-American leaders were calling attention to the case, and the national media then picked up the story, portraying Martin as an African-American martyr who was killed because Zimmerman picked on him due to racial profiling. Public perception quickly gelled of Zimmerman as a prejudiced racial profiler who had targeted an innocent victim walking through the community because of his skin color. Only later did media images surface of Zimmerman with wounds he previously claimed he received at the hands of Martin, and Zimmerman eventually was acquitted.[9]

More recent incidents have occurred with the death of Michael Brown in Ferguson, Missouri,[10] and Eric Garner in New York City,[11] both garnering significant attention by the national media before grand juries decided not to indict the police responsible for the killings. Both decisions sparked large protests. The media has helped to fuel the spreading outrage that is increasing racial tensions today and could even lead to further tension. The media might also have the ability to tamp down tensions by showing examples of different racial groups working together in peace and harmony in different arenas. But then, the stories of violence are what sells newspapers and glues viewers to the news on their television sets, the Internet, or iPhones. So since violence is a more interesting story to draw readers and viewers, that's what the media tends to emphasize. And so, even more recent incidents in Baltimore and Cleveland tended to play out similarly, but with perhaps a touch more sensitivity on all sides.

In all these cases, the media not only contributed to the portrayal of defendants as guilty before the trials even began, but they also played a role in inflaming race relations. These racial biases can operate against minority ethnic groups of any type, and could have been a factor in Carol's case, since she was identified in the minds of the kids and some community member as a "Nazi" due to her accent and repeated attempts to admonish them from doing something they liked to do.

Stereotyping

Stereotyping occurs all the time in crime news reporting. A pro-prosecution slant arises as local and wire service reporters have long-established relationships with law-enforcement agencies and prosecutors who "serve superiors with strong career incentives to maximize publicity for crime-fighting successes."[12] Therefore, as Entman and Gross point out: [Reporters engage in] an overreliance on public officials, overuse of standardized story scripts and familiar stereotypes, and 'pack journalism' — the tendency of reporters from nominally competitive news organizations to converge on the same framings. In the case of crime coverage, these media routines can facilitate a pro-prosecution slant that appears across news coverage when law-enforcement officials are eager to promote claims of guilt.

This use of stereotyping can be especially damaging for African-Americans and Latinos[12], as well as police.

Criminal Profiling

While racial profiling has been rightly accused of wrongly targeting suspects based on their racial or ethnic characteristics, *criminal profiling* is equally dangerous. Take the case of Richard Jewell, originally considered a hero for discovering a pipe bomb planted in a knapsack at the Centennial Olympic Park in Atlanta during the 1996 Summer Olympics. Jewell was working as a security guard when he discovered the bomb on park grounds, alerted the police, and helped evacuate people from the area before the bomb exploded, saving hundreds of people from death or injury. Initially, the press feted Jewell as a hero for his discovery and his quick thinking that saved many lives.[13]

However, three days after his discovery, Jewell became a suspect, for he fit an FBI "lone bomber" criminal profile. For the next three months after the *Atlanta Journal-Constitution* revealed the FBI viewed Jewell as a possible suspect due to this profile, Jewell's life became a living hell.

Reporters speculated Jewell was a "failed law enforcement officer who may have planted the bomb so he could find it and be a hero" ("Richard Jewell," *Wikipedia*, en.wikipedia.org/wiki/Richard Jewell). These reports led two of the bombing victims to file suits against Jewell, who consequently became the target of jokes on late-night TV.

The media and public pressure on Jewell only began to ease up after his attorneys hired an ex-FBI agent to administer a lie-detector test that he passed, at which time Jewell was formally cleared. Consequently, he prevailed in a series of suits against the media, including NBC News and the *New York Post,* for some of their remarks. Eventually, Jewell was completely exonerated when the real bomber, Eric R. Rudolph, pleaded guilty to the Olympic Park attack.[13]

In another notorious case of a press lynching, the press did it not just once, but twice, as after the first defendant proved innocent, they went after another. Unfortunately, this second individual killed himself, and was only to be shown as most likely innocent after his death. The case involves the anthrax mailings, which began in September 2001. Envelopes which contained spores of anthrax were mailed to several press organizations and two Democratic Senators. The envelopes were accompanied by letters that suggested they had been sent by an Arab extremist, or someone posing as one, since they included the statements, "We have this anthrax... Death to America... Death to Israel." The letters resulted in 17 people becoming ill and 5 deaths.[14]

The ensuing media coverage and copycat hoax mailings contributed to a sense of panic among the general population. Meanwhile, there was great pressure on the FBI and law enforcement to quickly apprehend the killer. It was in this climate that the FBI focused on the limited number of American scientists who might have a working knowledge of anthrax. One of these scientists was Steven Hatfill, a medical doctor, who had once worked at the Army's elite Medical Research Institute of Infectious Diseases (USAMRIID), which had stocks of anthrax. Instead of conducting a quiet exploratory investigation, as is common in the early stages of any investigation, the FBI did the opposite in the Hatfill case, conducting its search of the doctor's apartment accompanied by TV news cameras broadcasting the search live. This search precipitated what became a kind of media offensive in a "war" against Hatfill. Reporters and camera crews swarmed into Hatfill's apartment after he signed a consent form to let the FBI search, as he felt he had nothing to hide.

The fallout from the investigation and media coverage included Hatfill quickly losing his job for a large defense contractor — and no one else wanting to hire him. Attorney General John Ashcroft also publicly declared Hatfill to be a "person of interest." Soon afterwards, FBI agents grilled his friends, tapped his phone, and installed surveillance cameras outside the condo of his girlfriend — where he now lived due to his loss of income. As described by David Freed, in an *Atlantic* article appropriately titled "The Wrong Man":

> *The result was an unrelenting stream of inflammatory innuendo that dominated front pages and television news. Hatfill found himself trapped, the powerless central player in what Connolly (Hatfill's attorney) describes as 'a story about the two most powerful institutions in the United States, the government and the press, ganging up on an innocent man. It's Kafka.*[14]

Hatfill's own effort to hold a press conferences to proclaim his innocence after the searches of his apartment had no effect, and he became a virtual recluse who turned to drinking and had to stop reading newspapers altogether. He says what saved him from suicide was the fact he started to study old medical textbooks like he was back in school again; his dreams of his eventual payday when he would sue the Justice Department and the reporters and newspapers that defamed him; and a visit to Sri Lanka to help treat the victims of a huge tsunami.

Meanwhile, for all of the FBI efforts to investigate Hatfill for six years, the agents were unable to provide any firm evidence, and he was never indicted. Consequently, Hatfill then initiated a series of lawsuits. The government eventually settled for $5.8 million, and there was an out-of-court settlement with both *Vanity Fair* and *The Reader's Digest*.

The only thing that stopped the FBI-press barrage was when new investigators reexamined the evidence in the case in early 2007, at which time agents came to believe that Hatfill never really had access to the anthrax at USAMRIID. Their new target, Bruce Edward Ivins, was a microbiologist who worked at the center and had access to the anthrax virus. The FBI and media proceeded to give Ivins the same relentless treatment as they had given Hatfill. Like Hatfill, Ivins was soon out of his job at a lab where he had worked for twenty-eight years. Meanwhile, the press began looking into "the pathology of Ivins' life" and linked him, although speculatively, to the murders.

Unlike Hatfill, Ivins did not possess the necessary mental stamina to withstand the pressure. Suffering from depression and anxiety, he entered into a voluntary two-week stay at a psychiatric hospital. Two weeks later, he killed himself with an overdose of Tylenol. Even after his death, though, the press did not let up, suggesting Ivins's suicide was proof of his guilt.

As it turns out, Ivins may not have been the real anthrax killer either. In July 2011, the Department of Justice filed court documents claiming that Ivins did not possess the equipment necessary to have conducted the attacks. In short, the FBI, along with the media, targeted not one, but two, innocent victims in the anthrax attacks, and the relentless media coverage helped destroy Stephen Hatfill's career and took Bruce Edwards Ivins's life.[14]

Perhaps the worst bias against defendants is that accorded by pundits in the media. According to Entman and Gross, certain opinion columnists and cable television personalities are "far and away the worst offenders in framing from a one-side prosecution perspective." They cite cable talk shows such as *The Nancy Grace Show* as the "most egregiously imbalanced."[12]

HOW TO DO IT BETTER

Unfortunately, rather than socially responsible journalism, much of what poses as journalistic writing and news reporting is designed to excite and titillate readers with slanted news and exposés about defendants. Then, once captured by the media headlights, such stories — whether true, false, or exaggerated — can be blasted everywhere.

Journalists need to recognize and take stock of the harm that can be done to defendants and their families, especially ones that eventually prove innocent. Likewise, broadcasters need to present more balanced news stories and include in-depth stories about criminal justice subjects, so people can better understand the biases woven through the criminal justice system and put pressure on their legislators to correct them.

By 2013, there were some indications from television and movies that more attention is being given to flaws in the criminal justice system, even if primarily from a liberal perspective. A *Charlie Rose* episode featured a panel discussion on prison reform that involved author Michelle Alexander and filmmaker Eugene Jarecki[15] and an *Independent Lens* episode on PBS featured a Eugene Jarecki documentary.[16] A *60 Minutes* episode featured the case of Michael Morton, wrongly convicted of his wife's murder and exonerated after twenty-five years in prison.[17,18] In addition, two movies, *West of Memphis*[19] and *Central Park Five*"[20] featured stories of two groups of juveniles — one white and the other black — convicted of serious crimes (murder, rape) they did not commit.

As African-Americans tend to identify with black victims and black defendants — and whites do the same with white defendants and white victims — there was a real need to more effectively balance the racial composition of juries in racially charged cases. However, the potentially inflammatory nature of these cases also requires the media to act in a more socially conscious fashion. They should take on more responsibility to report such cases with restraint. In short, the media needs to avoid pouring kerosene on the fire at any point in these — and all — cases.

Here are some ways the media might be called to account, resulting in a more responsible, reliable reporting, based on presenting stories that are based on the facts, rather than sensationalized stories where gossip and innuendo turn innocent victims into criminals without any proof that they are:

- Names of individuals charged with a crime should not be reported by the media. Reports should mention only that the individuals have been apprehended and whether they were released on bail. This anonymity should also remain the case during and after a trial unless the trial results in a guilty verdict.

- Media should not be allowed to report what they learn from prosecutors unless the defense lawyers are also allowed to comment on that information.

- Reporters, publishers, and producers who have produced false stories should be required to do follow-up stories, apart from any other penalties, to make up for the vilification. They should do these follow-ups within a certain date of their offense in telling a false story, and this story should be placed on the first page of a newspaper or in the first 3 to 5 minutes of a news story on TV or the Internet media.

- The publishers and owners of the broadcast and Internet media should be held more closely responsible for the stories printed or posted in their media, so that they could be held liable civilly or criminally, along with reporters for false or sensationalized stories. The liability for false and sensationalized stories might be extended beyond the harm done to a particular individual or organization when the story leads to widespread protests that cause more extensive damages, such as to a community whose neighborhood is trashed by a protest sparked by a false story.

- The standard for a reporter or publication might be changed from reporting what is simply alleged or rumored to reporting what is actually known or making it very clear that there is a lack of actual facts in a case — not just simply using the term "alleged" to permit the attribution of false and damaging claims to an individual or organization.

CHAPTER 15: THE PROBLEM WITH THE POLICE

Only about 1% of police officers are subject to misconduct complaints, though it is difficult to obtain accurate statistics since neither the government nor police agencies regularly collect such data. However, some "cop watch" groups do. The Cato Institute's National Police Misconduct Reporting Project's 2010 report[1] cited 4,861 reports of police misconduct throughout the nation. Only 33% of the criminal cases brought against these police officers resulted in convictions, with 36% of those convictions resulting in incarcerations.

The Cato Project report ultimately concluded that the police are more likely than the average person to commit a number of crimes, among them assault, sexual assault and murder. It estimated that about 1 in 4.7 officers will be involved in some act of misconduct during their careers.[1] Still, any such misconduct may go unreported and thus be underestimated for two reasons. First, is the "police code of silence," whereby individual officers will not turn each other in, even if they observe another officer behaving badly, and second, many victims of police abuse don't file complaints.

One of the most famous cases of police misconduct happened back in the late 1990s. At that time, more than seventy LAPD officers assigned to the Rampart Division with the Community Resources Against Street Hoodlums (CRASH) anti-gang unit were implicated in some form of misconduct. Among these were "unprovoked shootings, unprovoked beatings, planting of false evidence, framing of suspects, sealing and dealing narcotics, bank robbery, perjury, and covering up of evidence of these activities."[2,3]

Eventually, fifty-eight officers were brought before an internal administrative board, but only twenty-four were actually found to have engaged in wrongdoing — and of these, twelve were given suspensions of various lengths, seven resigned or retired, and five were fired. Still, the repercussions were huge. Because of falsified evidence and police perjury, 106 prior criminal convictions were overturned and more than 140 civil lawsuits were filed against the city of Los Angeles costing the city about $125 million in settlements.[4] Fortunately, since that time, the LAPD has undergone much reform under Chief William Bratton, currently NYPD Commissioner.

Police Misconduct and Abuse

Two major laws are designed to facilitate communications between the police and citizens who seem suspicious, or whose actions give rise to a belief they may have illegal property or weapons. However, it is relatively easy for the police to misuse these laws.

Stop and Identify

The stop-and-identify laws are statutes that allow police to detain people and ask them to identify themselves, commonly by showing an ID. If the individuals refuse to properly identify themselves or show a false ID, the police are in their rights to arrest them. However, if a police officer simply stops to chat with someone for just a "contact" or "conversation," that person *is* free to not respond, or leave the conversation. It is if and when the police decide that a person is not free to go that such a conversation/contact becomes "a detention" — and that is when the laws about stop and identify (and arrest) come into play.

A common problem is that citizens can be confused about when a conversation ends and a detention begins, since at any time a police officer can approach a person to ask them questions. For example: An encounter may begin if the officer suspects someone is involved in a crime, but does not yet possess the "specific and articulable facts" that could justify that person's detention or arrest. The criteria that need to be met to justify a detention are vague, and so the police are often able to claim the right to question based on ambiguous "facts" — facts that could fit nearly any person in the area as their criteria! Consider, for example, if the police are using a description of a suspect as "a tall African-American male" as the basis for their questioning, and yet this "fact" could fit nearly any male living or walking in the area. This then can result in racial profiling.

The original statutes about detention go back to *Terry v. Ohio*.[5] It gave local and state police the ability to briefly detain a person if they have a "…reasonable suspicion that the person has committed, is committing, or is about to commit a crime." Under *Terry*, the police can conduct a limited search for weapons (a "frisk") if they *reasonably* suspect that the person to be detained may be armed and dangerous.[6] But abuse occurs when police officers use the laws covering detention in conjunction with racial profiling, or with targeting people who live in an area known for a high rate of crime. Here, the police may not have any specific information that a particular person is involved in a crime, but they still may stop that person on the street anytime for questioning. In fact, it has become commonplace nowadays that police frequently detain those living in inner city areas for such questioning, perhaps up to several times a day. Mere failure to identify oneself can merit jail time up to a year or steep fines in certain jurisdictions.[7]

Often abuse occurs in those cities and states where, for example, there is a large Hispanic population, and police are using the stop-and-identify laws in order to check and see if a person is an illegal immigrant. If the person is, they then may turn the individual over to the Immigration and Naturalization Service (INS). In other areas, the police might be using the stop-and-identify laws to target someone believed to be on parole or probation to investigate them further — even if the individual is not doing anything illegal at that specific point — and then find a reason to make an arrest. A scathing report was recently issued on the Ferguson, Missouri police force by the Department of Justice for civil offenses of this sort against blacks.[8]

So in short, police officers have used and are using the stop- and-identify laws to target and harass a particular individual or class of defendants based on racial profiling, given the discretion of the police to interpret terms such as "reasonable suspicion," "probable cause," and "articulable facts."

Search and Seizure

There is also a potential for police misconduct at the point when a detention turns into *an arrest*. While the standard for a detention is a *reasonable suspicion* that a person is involved or may be involved in criminal activity, an arrest requires *probable cause,* or "enough reliable information" to "support a reasonable belief that a person has committed a crime." When an arrest occurs, the police now are able to search a person as well their belongings and immediate surroundings. If police have insufficient evidence, they may be tempted to arrest without probable cause, which then allows them to search for more evidence, albeit illegally. If the person arrested hires an attorney afterwards, the lawyer can claim the search was illegal, which could result in the evidence thrown out. Yet many times those arrested who have a low-income status cannot afford to hire a lawyer to file such a motion.

Based on the Fourth Amendment, the police cannot unreasonably seize people or their property. They cannot act on a hunch, pretext, or hope they will catch a criminal. They must have *reliable* information. They must have *probable cause,*[9] as defined earlier.

A police officer can conduct such a search with or without a warrant. To obtain a warrant, the officer needs probable cause and must make a statement signed under oath to the judge in which they state the facts. Then, the search must be made within the boundaries of the search warrant.[9] For example, if the warrant provides a right to search a suspect's garage, it does not give the police the right to also search the suspect's house (although the police might uncover evidence that gives them probable cause to search other areas).

Searches can also take place without a warrant, which is where the potential for abuse really comes into play:

- If a police officer makes a legitimate arrest, the officer can make a search "incident to arrest" of both the suspect and immediate area around the suspect.
- If a police officer sees evidence of a crime or illegal contraband in plain view from an area where a police officer already has a right to be, they can seize it.
- If there is an urgent situation — such as a strong possibility the evidence of a crime will be destroyed or a suspect will escape — then an officer is permitted to conduct a warrantless search.

On face value, these laws seem reasonable. *But police officers can easily stretch the definitions and descriptions in these laws to search and seize just about anything.* Those subjected to these policies have little recourse, since they are already detained, arrested, or have provided consent (albeit reluctantly). And, illegal searches can only be challenged in the future by attorneys — whom, again, many defendants cannot afford to hire. Too, if the defendant and police subsequently offer different accounts of what transpired, judges and juries are inclined to believe the officer.

The reality is such issues of police misconduct primarily take place in the inner cities, as a police department in a lower-income area of a city may be apt to disrespect the rights of local citizens whom they may perceive as part of a culture of crime. In contrast, a police department in the suburbs that deals primarily with middle and upper-income individuals is likely to be more respectful to its citizens, who can more easily afford to hire lawyers if misconduct occurs.

Police Brutality

Police brutality can also be an example of police misconduct. We will not deal with police brutality here, except to state that there have been many recent examples, such as the case of Eric Garner, who died as a result of a chokehold by a police officer,[11] and even more recent shootings in Baltimore and Cleveland.

Incentives for Police Misconduct

Arrests and convictions prove particularly easy in inner city neighborhoods where drugs are openly bought and sold on the streets. One reason police target minorities in these areas is that they are rewarded by both pay and promotions based on the numbers of arrests and convictions they make. And it is far easier to make arrests that lead to convictions or pleas in drug possession cases than in murder cases, which require substantially more investigative efforts.[10]

Incentives such as these contribute significantly to police misconduct. And although many police departments have citizen police review boards where individuals can bring complaints, the complaints can be hard to prove when they are basically "he said/she said" cases in which the word of one officer is pitted against the word of a private individual.

Is there Effective Recourse against Police Misconduct?

At the Federal Level

Federal laws enable a person to file a complaint against police with the U.S. Department of Justice (DOJ), but there are severe limitations.

Typically, criminal and civil cases are investigated and handled separately, even if they arise out of the same incident. In a criminal case, the DOJ brings a case against the accused person in order to punish that person — something that requires a higher standard of evidence. While the DOJ does not function as a victim's lawyer, it may call the victim as a witness in the rare event it decides to prosecute.

By contrast, in a civil case, the DOJ brings its case through litigation or through conducting an administrative investigation against a government authority or law enforcement agency. In such civil suits, the DOJ "seeks to correct a law enforcement agency's policies and practices that fostered the misconduct." Sometimes, there will be additional relief awarded for the victim(s) of the misconduct. However, a single incident of misconduct is not enough to bring a case, for it must be part of a "pattern or practice," as recently shown in the DOJ report on Ferguson, Missouri.[8] The DOJ has to show in court that "the agency has an unlawful policy or that the incidents constituted a pattern of unlawful conduct." The main remedy under this law is to secure injunctive relief to end the misconduct and change the agency's policies and procedures that resulted in or allowed it to occur. Unfortunately, there is no provision for the victims of the misconduct to receive any personal monetary relief, and the victim cannot initiate any litigation under this law.

The DOJ typically has a high conviction rate in any cases it brings against citizens, but only a few of the police misconduct cases make it through the DOJ review process. For example, of 10,129 cases the DOJ reviewed, only 2,619 were investigated. Only 79 civil rights cases were filed, of which only 22 were official misconduct cases, including police abuse.[12] This means *less than 0.2% of the more than ten thousand civil cases reviewed resulted in official misconduct cases filed for prosecution:*

> Not only are police misconduct cases prosecuted at
> the lowest rate among civil rights prosecutions, but
> civil rights offenses themselves are prosecuted less
> than any other category of offense handled by the U.S.
> Justice Department.[12]

There are two main factors behind this. First, there are only a small number of attorneys working in the DOJ's Civil Rights Division. Out of the 9,168 attorneys employed by the DOJ in 1997, there were only 32 full-time attorneys in the Criminal Section of the Civil Rights Division — the office responsible for prosecuting police and other official misconduct cases.[12]

The second problematic factor is that DOJ prosecutors rely on the FBI to conduct inquiries into allegations of criminal civil rights violations. However, the typical FBI investigation of police abuse complaints is limited to information provided by the local law enforcement agency itself, and such information is "…routinely inadequate or biased." Moreover, since DOJ rules require that the preliminary FBI report be submitted within a mere twenty-one days, the short deadline reduces the likelihood the FBI has enough time to conduct a thorough investigation.[12] The end result is that the DOJ is unable to effectively and efficiently prosecute police misconduct cases.

At the State and Local Level

Citizens can make a complaint of police misconduct locally to police departments' internal affairs division, or to their local community police review board. However, such review boards tend to be overwhelmed with cases of police misconduct. As a result, the boards are often behind on reviewing the cases submitted to them, and consequently only deal with a small percentage of cases. By the time a review panel brings up a case for review at a public hearing, the original complainant may have lost interest in pursuing the matter or has moved elsewhere, and a large percentage of cases are closed without review. Then, too, many of these boards operate in opposition to police groups like the local police union, so often the officers cited do not show up for the hearing(s), which results in postponements. Consequently, a complainant who initially appears for a hearing may lose interest in showing up again.

Police Backlash

Lately, the public is collecting and revealing evidence of police misconduct and abuse through video and audio recordings that provide a record of what really happened in instances of alleged police misconduct. For example, there was a video taken of the in-the-back shooting of citizen Oscar Grant at an Oakland, CA station (featured in the recent movie *Fruitvale Station*. Eventually, Bay Area Rapid Transit (BART) Officer Mehserle, who claimed he had mistakenly drawn his gun instead of a Taser, was found guilty of involuntary manslaughter, and BART settled with the mother of Grant's daughter for $1.5 million.[13] A more recent example would be the Eric Garner case.[11]

In response to the growing use of digital recording devices by the public, there has been a police backlash — resulting in the police recording the citizens recording them. The police have used eavesdropping and wiretapping laws to charge citizens who record them without their knowledge.[14]

Some citizens even have been subject to jail terms because of recording police misconduct. For instance, in Illinois, a citizen who records audio of police officers without their consent can be charged with a Class 1 felony that has a prison term of up to fifteen years.

More commonly though, the police have responded to citizens trying to record them by using ambiguous charges; for example, they might claim that the citizen is "interfering with a police officer, refusing to obey a lawful order, or obstructing an arrest or police action." In other cases, police may illegally confiscate cameras, delete evidence, or incorrectly tell citizens they are not allowed to film. However, when citizens are able to record and keep their audios or videos, even surreptitiously, they have played an important role in making the public aware of police misconduct. The video recording of the police shooting of Walter Scott in North Charleston, S.C. in 2015, resulting in a murder charge against the police officer, is one such incident. Indeed, many police departments are now recording more incidents themselves with cameras mounted on officers or police cars.

HOW TO DO IT BETTER

Some suggestions to rein in abuses by the police include the following:

- *Create a national clearinghouse for reports by citizen-police review boards.* Members of Congress could introduce legislation to fund this organization. The organization could review any complaints in a timely fashion and provide a national record of complaints that could be accessed by citizens everywhere. Such a database would keep police misconduct from being "buried" in local files.
- *Develop national training guidelines and policies for police departments nationwide*—a "code of conduct" that local police departments could follow in order to improve police operations, increase compliance, and reduce citizen complaints against the police. The clearinghouse above could facilitate this.
- *Local citizen review boards could include some members of the local board of supervisors* (a governing body in many cities composed of representatives chosen by district or citywide elections). Increasing citizen involvement on these boards would improve awareness and accountability. With little community-wide participation present in these boards as of this writing, the boards are often ignored by the police department internal affairs divisions, which tend to support the police version of events and are influenced by the police "code of silence". More community support and awareness of these review boards might come about

through more outreach to the local communities, such as by establishing a regular column in a local paper or weekly blog. Citizen review boards also might actively search out community leaders to get them involved. For example, board members might promote citizen participation at such local business groups as that city's chamber of commerce.

- *A training program might be developed to increase police awareness of local community needs and how officers could better interact with local citizens in a spirit of trust and cooperation.* This program might be designed or selected by a team of consultants who already work as advisors to the police departments. In such a training program, police officers would be shown how to better understand the main types of complaints against them and how to change their behavior to reduce such complaints in the future.

- *There should be an expanded and mandatory use of new technologies, such as audio recordings when a police officer stops or arrests a citizen, and recording videos from small cameras attached to a police officer's uniform.* These recordings could prove useful should there be contradictory accounts by a police officer and a citizen.

- *Remove any restrictions on the public in terms of on filming and recording the police when they are on duty.* This permission to record will provide the necessary transparency to show how the police engage with citizens. Such technology would dissuade any police officers from later making false claims about how a citizen responded to an arrest or other action(s).

- *The Department of Justice should provide its Civil Rights Division with more attorneys so that it can pursue more cases, and require the FBI to perform its own independent investigations of police misconduct rather than rely on information provided by the police.*

CHAPTER 16: COLLATERAL DAMAGE TO FAMILIES

Generally, the term *collateral damage* refers to unintended damage from a military operation, which can include the destruction of civilians, buildings, and properties not related to mission objectives. *Collateral damage* may also be applied to any case that goes through the criminal justice system, as the process impacts entire family units — spouses, children, parents, and relatives — and all of the defendant's relationships. Such unintended consequences occur at all stages of a prosecution, from the initial charge, to the trial and verdict. If the charged person is found guilty, these consequences continue to happen during that person's probation or imprisonment.

But even if the result is a not-guilty verdict, there still is collateral damage. For instance, once a person is charged with a crime, everyone related to that individual can experience a huge financial, emotional, mental, and physical toll. Whether or not a defendant actually goes to prison, the damages to the lifestyle and the career of a partner or family member can be considerable. And as the potential for the defendant's long sentence mounts, the feeling of unfairness on the family's part can lead to significant anger and hurt — emotions that do not simply disappear when a charged individual is found innocent. Regrettably, these everyday side effects of our judicial system have largely been ignored.

The Impact on Families

On a Personal Note

Once my loved one was accused, I became collateral damage. As Carol suffered, I felt it. I felt her anger. I felt her despair. I felt her justifiable indignation. And there was nothing I seemed to be able to do to protect her, which made me feel inadequate and worthless. My sense of personal worth suffered further as I came to realize there should have been times when I offered Carol even more support.

The damage to our finances, while more minor at the start, became extensive and excessive. We lost our cherished no-commute lifestyle. We had to sell our home.

My relationship with Carol suffered both during and after her ordeal. She became emotionally fragile, withdrawn, and depressed. This had gone on for a period of over five years, and it affected me intensely. As her husband, I had to contend with these difficult changes — it wasn't easy.

I experienced great setbacks in my work as well. I had to take a lot of time off to help care for my wife and fight the unjust charges against her. It threw my professional career into disarray. For a time, I virtually had to abandon my work to assist Carol in contending with the system and to provide her with emotional support. Very few in my department at the time extended any emotional support or understanding, and since the ordeal, my attempts to revive my research work have been slow and haphazard.

As our ordeal progressed, I found it very difficult to continue working in an environment where Carol and I got such little support. For a time, I considered ending my career in scientific research.

I changed as a person too. I grew resentful: of the media, of my colleagues, and of my community for not caring to hear our side of the story; for presuming Carol was guilty if they heard of the incident; and for their lack of support.

Instead of relaxing and moving comfortably towards retirement, I am spending time and effort writing this book in an attempt to put the past behind us; to make our side of the story clear and transparent; and to fix flaws in our judicial system so that others do not experience the same direct and/or collateral damage.

A Loss of Privacy

When a case goes to trial or otherwise gets media attention, everyone in a family is affected. Friends and neighbors often respond differently than before or turn a cold shoulder. Children get teased or taunted at school. Relatives may get suspicious. Strangers get nosy. In short, life is no longer the same.

Jon Benet Ramsey's parents were subjected to a witch-hunt and media frenzy for many years, all because of the suspicions that John Ramsey had killed his six-year-old daughter, a beauty pageant queen. Eventually, to gain some sort of privacy and escape the media's unrelenting glare, John and his wife Patsy sold their home in Colorado and moved out of state. Yet even there, the media, intent on keeping the national story alive, haunted the couple. It was not until 2008 — after Patsy Ramsey's death from cancer — that John Ramsey was no longer considered a suspect. At this time, the Boulder District Attorney formally apologized to him and his family for the "cloud of suspicion" they had to endure for over a decade. [1]

Psychological Damage/Familial Fall-Out

Several aspects of a criminal case can produce long-term negative psychological damage for the entire family. For children especially, the process of taking the accused away can be particularly unsettling. And if police come to the family home to make an arrest or further investigate after arresting a family member, they may tear apart the residence looking for potential evidence to add to their case. While the police are initially limited to just the areas of the house under the control of the individual they have arrested, they can search further. Ultimately, they may find a reason to search the whole house. If this occurs, family members and/or others only can look on helplessly, unable to halt the process. Chances are, bedrooms are invaded or journals and computers are reviewed and perhaps even taken for evidence.

Family members can feel unnerved if they get a call from the accused, with typically the first call being from jail to say they have been arrested. During that conversation, the accused may ask them to quickly get bail together to get them out of jail. But if the family doesn't have immediate access to the full amount requested, they may have to pay a bail bondsman 10% of the total. If adequate financial resources are not available, then they must meet with the accused in jail, where they, too, feel they are subjected to degradation and humiliation.

If the accused manages to return home, family members can still feel quite unnerved and vulnerable by what has happened. Unhappily, this is only the beginning. Family members will be called upon to do even more. For instance, they feel a need to appear at a series of hearings, as well as find and meet with a lawyer to help their loved one.

Far worse still is collateral damage to families of those in prison.

Even greater fall-out for families and children is the feelings of shame and social stigma that comes having a family member in prison. Many family members don't tell even their closest friends if a family member is in prison, doing whatever they can to maintain this family "secret."

Virtually no support is available for the families of individuals processed through the criminal justice system. As author Creasie Finney Hairston points out, the fallout for families has long been largely ignored:

> *The well-being of prisoners' families and children has not been an important part of this social policy agenda... services and activities that assist prisoners in carrying out family roles and responsibilities have seldom been included in the strategic plans of social service agencies or corrections departments.* [2]

Moreover, visiting the person imprisoned can be traumatic, discouraging families from wanting to visit again:

> *For many families and friends of prisoners, the visit to a prison is a lesson in humility, intimidation and frustration and a highly charged and anxiety producing event. It is not unusual for visitors, the majority of whom are women and children to endure many indignities.... long waits sometimes in facilities without seating, toilets, and water; the lack of nutritious food in visiting room vending machines and the absence of activities for children. Body frisks and intrusive searches, rude treatment by staff, and hot, dirty and crowded visiting rooms are the norm in many prisons. Visitors may be denied entry to the prison for diverse reasons including constantly changing dress codes, no identification for children, and ion drug scanners that inaccurately signal that a visitor is carrying drugs.* [2]

Some incarcerated parents prefer that their children not visit them in prison or make any effort to contact them, commonly because they are embarrassed or ashamed and feel the visit will hurt their child more. They may ask other family members to keep their imprisonment secret in order to "protect" their child.

At the same time, many corrections and social services professionals discourage prison visits by children, because they are concerned about the effect of the oppressive prison environment on the underaged and legitimately concerned such children may come to accept incarceration as "normal." [2]

Deterioration of Family Units

Many state laws allow for *the termination of parental rights solely on the basis of criminal activity*[3] — which means those states can place any children in state custody and effectively break up the family. Alternatively, parental rights can also be terminated if "parents fail to communicate regularly with their children."[2]

Marital or romantic relationships can suffer significant, sometimes insurmountable, damage for a variety of reasons. When someone is imprisoned, the resulting physical and emotional separation from loved ones becomes a key factor in divorces, breakups for unmarried couples, disruptions in parenting, and child custody battles that devastate both parents and children. As Hairston notes:

> *Couples are usually denied sexual intimacy and are unable to engage in the day-to-day interactions, experiences and sharing which sustain marital and other intimate, adult relationships. Loneliness and missing each other and a host of other feelings about the separation, justice system, criminal activity, and each partner's honesty and faithfulness are common.*[2]

Financial Woes

Another huge problem that soon may arise is financial. Not only must prisoners' families deal with the high toll of the incarcerated individual's loss of income, but also those families who try to keep regular contact with a prisoner experience:

> *...the costs of maintaining the household, the loss of income of the imprisoned parent who was contributing to the household, legal fees associated with criminal defense and appeals, the costs associated with maintaining contact during imprisonment and the costs of maintaining the prisoner while he (or she) is in prison.*[2]

Maintaining contact with the person in prison can be expensive, since prison visits are very costly due to the family's need for transportation (often to a remote location), meals, vending machine snacks; and perhaps the cost of a hotel or motel for those visiting overnight. Family too must pay for something as necessary and commonplace as the prisoner's phone calls. Unable to own cell phones in prison and denied Internet access, prisoners can only call collect, and this can rack up big bills. Low-income families normally cannot afford these costs, especially if the prisoner was the primary source of support for the family.

Family members of incarcerated prisoners may need to take on roles previously played by the incarcerated family member. They may pitch in and help out, or take on full or major responsibility for something the incarcerated family member used to routinely handle, such as being the primary breadwinner. Grandmothers, sisters, and aunts might take on the childrearing responsibilities of a prisoner's young children; spouses may need to take on extra work to support the family.[2]

Those relatives who take care of the children of mothers or fathers in prison undergo additional financial expenses, as it falls to them to supply the children with food, clothing, any necessary daycare, and/or transportation arrangements to get the kids to school.[2]

Other expenses families of incarcerated individuals must bear include the costs to provide prisoners with everyday items not provided by the prison. These include toiletries, reading materials, stamps, food, and clothing. The prisoners also pay indirectly for other services, such as when the prison places a levy on funds in their account, deposited for any paid work they do, for medical visits, health care, institutional fines and child support.[2]

Without the prisoner's financial contribution, some families may seek outside assistance, such as Medicaid, relative foster care payments, or public assistance welfare benefits. However, the reality is some choose not to seek this outside assistance even if they need it, as it exposes the family to "external scrutiny," which can risk an official action (such as the authorities removing the children from the homes of the relatives and friends who are caring for them and placing the kids in foster care).

The consequences of lockups therefore are horrendous for prisoners' families, and all too often families become incentivized to break up, due to the high cost of maintaining contact and supporting a prisoner in prison. Thus, incarceration erodes family values.

A Family's Future Picture, Financial and Otherwise

According to some studies, many inmates often start to withdraw from being actively involved in their children's lives if they discover their former partner has started a new relationship. At the same time, mothers whose partners are in prison often choose new boyfriends who are abusive, something that ultimately can cost them custody of their own children. Besides suffering from the decline in family income from a parent in prison, mothers and their children can face further economic difficulties. Often the families of incarcerated fathers cut off any financial assistance to the mother if the mother has given up on the father as a partner. This cut-off of funds can then lead mothers to depression and prostitution, something that further traumatizes the children.[4]

Another indirect, but very real, form of collateral damage for families is the loss of income that occurs when a defendant who has a professional or business license is no longer able to practice in that profession or run that business. Oftentimes, defendants plead guilty to a lesser felony, not realizing it could jeopardize their chances of future employment.

Often, convicted defendants lose their licenses or find it difficult to secure employment after they have paid their dues, despite laws that encourage employers to not discriminate against previously convicted employees.

Moreover, there are other "wide ranging prohibitions and disqualifications that often face ex-offenders upon the completion of criminal sentences." For example, in Arizona, ex-cons are blocked from public and housing benefits and face restrictions on employment and voting. The irony is that these additional consequences generally last longer than the direct sentence, so these restrictions often impose harsher and longer lasting penalties than the original sentence did. Too, since the consequences are not part of the formal sentencing process, defendants, defense lawyers, and judges may not even think about them at the time of sentencing. The result is that many criminal defendants plead guilty to criminal offenses without any awareness of the serious consequences that will affect their future daily life. These consequences affect the defendants *and their families.* There also may be barriers to accessing the safety net provided by many social service programs, most needed when ex-offenders are first released."[5] Thus the consequences of a person's conviction are severe for the vast majority of families of ex-convicts, who consequently struggle mightily to re-establish themselves in society.

The process is equally hard on the families of defendants who plead guilty to a lesser crime, in the false belief this provides an easy way out of the criminal justice system. This plea only places them into a more vulnerable position due to the denial of many benefits they might otherwise receive. For example, getting a commercial driver's license, possessing a firearm, and even voting are also all prohibited for ex-convicts, and a convicted parent may find it more difficult to obtain joint custody after a divorce.[5]

Damage to the Children

Children are especially affected, many of whom suffer long-lasting negative outcomes related to their health, academic achievement, and behavior. While it may be financially and emotionally advantageous for spouses to break up, the children may be further hurt and traumatized by having (potentially) little to no contact with their incarcerated parent. Minority, and particularly black, families are disproportionately affected in this way because their rates of incarcerated family members are so high.

According to *Prisoners Once Removed* [4], the ways the children are impacted include:

- Children experience the loss of a parent as a traumatic event, and they suffer under the stigma of having a parent in prison, bearing it as a badge of shame and withdrawing from most social relationships. As a result, sometimes a mother won't tell the children that their father has been incarcerated — although they may find out later from peers or other adults, which generally is more traumatic for them than hearing it from their parent.

- Children frequently are unable to cope with their father's incarceration, and express their feelings of fear, anxiety, and anger by doing badly at school (they are twice as likely to drop out if their father is not present) and by engaging in anti-social behavior, such as stealing and starting fires.

- Just as the partner of the incarcerated prisoner may become depressed, children of depressed parents are eight times more likely to become depressed themselves (and to remain that way into adulthood!).

- Children typically find visits to a prison unpleasant, which further strains family ties by providing negative incentives to visit.

- In addition, the 40% of children of incarcerated parents who are adolescents (aged 10-17) often exhibit conduct problems predictive of future adult criminality, and "the chances that a young man will engage in criminal activity doubles if he is raised without a father." [6]

- Some relevant statistics include that 2% of all minor children have a parent in prison; [7] that during the first four months of a father's absence, the chances that the child's family falls below the poverty line doubles from 18.5% to 37.5%; [4] that less than 3% of these children go to college compared to 39.6% of others; [8] and that in 2012, 51% of 16-19 year old children of incarcerated parents were unemployed compared to 23.7% of those in the general population.[9]

- Children of incarcerated parents are more likely to experience family and residential instability, and end up in the foster care system more often than other children. (*"Families with Incarcerated Parents Fact Sheet,"* Second Chance Coalition Principle).

HOW TO DO IT BETTER

What can be done to alleviate the real burden and hurts families of convicted defendants face? We suggest:

- *Extra counseling, tutoring, and mentoring support through the schools to children of incarcerated parents.* This could help head off the likely problems of poor school performance and bad behavior. Group counseling could help these kids know they're not alone.

- *Support programs for the wives and children of returning prisoners, much like for families of returning soldiers, to help them better know what difficulties to expect.* If informed as to any potential employment or licensing difficulties in advance, family members can better help the formerly incarcerated parent adjust to these new realities.

- *A program through which partners of prisoners could form small groups to take care of each other's children when at work or during prison visits and support staff at the jails to help visitors take care of their children*

- *Expansion of re-entry and job training for prisoners and ex-prisoners to help them successfully re-enter normal society.* Such training might include help with finding jobs, acquiring new skills or updating old ones, and placement programs to tutor prisoners so they perform better in job interviews and advise them about searching websites such as www.indeed.com. It might also provide support groups for prisoners re-entering society so they can share their experiences.

- *New prison parenting programs to help prisoners remain in good contact with their children, and programs to help ex-prisoners return to parenting and re-establish a good, solid relationship with their children upon their return.*

- *Engage community-based agencies, such as volunteer and faith-based organizations, to provide prisoners and ex-convicts with institutional job-skills programs.* For example, The Project Return,[10] a community-inspired project started by five ministers in Nashville as a 501 (c)(3) Nonprofit Organization, offers pre-release and job-readiness classes, and then some post-conviction programs, including housing referrals, emergency food boxes, purchasing and providing work tools, transportation (metro Nashville transit bus passes,) clothing referrals (i.e., Salvation Army, Dress for Success), medical referrals (i.e., substance abuse, mental health, etc.), and assistance with securing birth certificates, ID cards, and Social Security cards. Such programs would likely be much better coordinated than any offered by federal or state bureaucracies, where turf wars would result in redundancy of effort and little effective coordination.

- *A path to reduce the automatic licensing restrictions that limit the jobs ex-cons can take without jeopardizing the rights of employers.* For example, on a case-by-case basis, ex-cons could apply for an exemption wherein they can submit letters of recommendations to remove their restriction on a provisional basis, while letting the employer know this has been removed. After six months of successfully performing the work subject to the restrictive license, the restriction could be removed permanently unless the ex-con is convicted for something again.

- *New sentencing policies could be put in place for nonviolent offenders to keep them out of prison or provide a shortened prison term,* such as by sentencing them to participate in community-based work-related programs that permit offenders with families to live at home or visit children on a regular basis. Another possibility might involve using community volunteer credits to offset a sentence, and imposing a suspended sentence that only results in imprisonment if the offender offends again.

CHAPTER 17: A NATIONAL SHAME: OUR CRIMINAL JUSTICE SYSTEM

One out of every 32 Americans — approximately 7.2 million adults as of this writing — is on probation, on parole, or in prison at any given time. In what has been described as the prison-industrial complex, approximately 2.3 million Americans are in prison, nearly one in one hundred adults.[1] We have 5% of the world's population, yet 25% of the world's prisoners.[2]

Ours is the highest rate of incarceration in the world — higher than Russia, China, or Iran. Eight times higher than the rate in Germany. And eight times higher than we had ourselves thirty years ago.[3] Who was watching? Not us.

To most of us, prisons are invisible. As Eugene Jarecki pointed out on a 2012 *Charlie Rose* program, the public is largely unaware of the prison situation because prisons are located in rural areas and the prison population is relatively powerless.[4]

It's enormously expensive to incarcerate so many people

The costs of incarceration, parole, and probation in the corrections "industry" amount to over $70 billion annually.[5] This is as much as the food stamp program.[6] State governments are strapped and increasingly concerned with the costs of incarcerating so many. The Republican governor of my state opted not to build a new prison and instead is sending inmates to a neighboring state, saving approximately $70 million in the process.

How did we get to this point? The Deleterious Effects of the War on Drugs

As Eugene Jarecki pointed out on the aforementioned Charlie Rose program, even employees in the criminal justice system, such as cops, judges, and prison guards, recognize that the drug war is not getting anywhere. *The drug war is taking money from budgets that could be better spent elsewhere.* There are perverse incentives in the system to keep this costly war going. For example, the officer who makes drug arrests gets overtime for doing the paperwork for each arrest. As a result, he can make many more arrests than an investigator who spends more time solving a homicide case. Thus, the cop who pursues the drug arrests is the one who gets promoted.[4]

This has blighted our inner cities. Rural counties where prisons are located gain more representation by having a larger population. However, the prisoners cannot vote, so their presence strengthens the voting power of the local population, which is primarily white. Those prisoners are removed from the areas where they used to live — usually the inner cities, which reduces the power of those areas. The growth of this industry is reflected in prison trade shows and in the pressure on local Congressmen to support prisons to bring business to a particular region.[4]

The war on drugs has failed to stop drug use or the spread of international gangs. As former Senator Jim Webb pointed out, "A dangerous form of organized and sometimes deadly gang activity has infiltrated America's towns and cities. It comes largely from our country's southern border, and much of the criminal activity centers around the movement of illegal drugs."[7] Much of this criminal activity comes from Mexican drug cartels, as they engage in extremely brutal actions to spread their profitable business enterprises through our cities.

Disproportionate Effects on Minority Communities

A serious side effect of the war on drugs is the perhaps unintended societal effects on minority communities. While the majority of illegal drug users and dealers throughout the U.S. are white, three-fourths of all the people incarcerated for drug offenses are African-Americans and Latinos. In 2006, one in nine 20-35 year old black men was behind bars, and far more were on probation or parole. In 2000, eight times as many whites were imprisoned for drug offenses as in 1983 (a huge increase); yet 22 times as many Latinos were imprisoned and 26 times as many African-Americans as in 1983.[3]

In some states, it's even worse:

> *In 2000... in seven states, African Americans constitute 80-90% of all drug offenders sent to prison. In at least 15 states, blacks are admitted to prison on drug charges at a rate from 20 to 57 times greater than that of white men.*[3]

The consequences include that African-American males are seven times more likely to be incarcerated than white males, that one out of fifteen African American men are in prison, compared to one out of thirty-six Hispanic men and one out of 106 white men, and that one in three black men will spend some time in prison during the course of their lifetime.[8] Furthermore, almost half, or 49.4%, of incarcerated parents are black, with African American children 7.5 times more likely and Hispanic children 2.5 times more likely than white children to have a parent in prison.[9] An article in *The New Yorker* even reported that, "In truth, there are more black men in the grip of the criminal-justice system — in prison, on probation, or on parole — than were in slavery."[10]

Civil rights advocate Michelle Alexander contends this happens in three phases:

1. Police apprehend more inner city blacks on drug charges because that is easier and more lucrative than arrests for other crimes, and they often employ racial profiling.
2. After their arrest, minority defendants generally do not receive legal representation due to their low-income status—and whether guilty or not, they are pressured to plead guilty and have to face harsh drug sentencing guidelines.
3. The laws that affect ex-cons' lives are debilitating since they deny employment, housing, education, and public benefits. Unable to surmount these obstacles, most ex-cons never reintegrate back into society and eventually return to prison. The recidivism rate for minority ex-cons is 70%.[3]

Once branded as felons, ex-cons face **legal discrimination** for the rest of their lives. They are barred from getting food stamps and obtaining public housing for themselves and their families. Whenever they apply for a job, they have to check a box as an indication they have been in prison. Our prison policy discourages stable relationships like marriage, which is particularly fragile in the African-American community. With many of the families of prisoners now living below the poverty line, U.S. welfare policy contributes to the problem by providing inadequate assistance to intact families. The AFDC (Aid to Families with Dependent Children) program unintentionally encourages African-American males to stay away from the home, too. All the way back in 1965, liberal Senator Daniel Patrick Moynihan identified the deleterious effects of this program, stating, "The steady expansion of this welfare program, as of public assistance programs in general, can be taken as a measure of the steady disintegration of the [African-American] family structure."[11]

The children of prisoners and ex-cons are increasingly troubled, and more likely to suffer from mental illness. They are likely to be poor, homeless, academically-challenged, and physically aggressive. Often they end up in prison themselves, continuing the vicious cycle. [12]

Something, obviously, is awry in America — one of the most "developed" countries in the world! *Why do we have such a high rate of incarceration in our nation? What can we do about it?*

HOW TO DO IT BETTER

Serious reform is needed for the prison system. This certainly won't be an easy fix, but there are ways that it is possible. *How can we do it better?*

- *Abolish mandatory minimum sentencing in cases of nonviolent drug cases.* Attorney General Holder made this recommendation in August 2013 after he acknowledged the huge prison population and its maintenance costs. This promising first step could reduce the prison population by several hundred thousand.

- *Set up re-entry centers to house prisoners in their last six months of incarceration.* These centers can train prisoners in life skills, handling finances, and job procurement at only about half the cost of a state's prison. [13]

- Rather than cutting back on the number of workers employed through the criminal justice system, *change the kinds of workers employed from a vast number of security guards (necessary as of this writing because of the massive amounts of prisoners in jail) to more counselors in mandated drug treatment facilities for convicts and newly released ex-cons.* Such a change might go a long way towards lowering the high recidivism rate for felons, and thus ultimately reduce violence on our streets and the high prison population.

- *By reducing the enormous costs of incarcerating prisoners who do not require imprisonment, funds could be released for many other worthwhile programs at the federal and state level.* This could include federal and state courts, both currently in serious financial difficulty. [14,15]

CHAPTER 18: EIGHT REMEDIES FOR OUR BROKEN CRIMINAL JUSTICE SYSTEM

In March 2009, Senator Webb issued a call for a national commission to engage in a complete overhaul of our criminal justice system. *This commission is needed now more than ever.* In particular, the commission should find answers to these key questions raised back then by Senator Webb:

- Why are there so many more Americans in prison compared with other countries and with our own history?
- What do our current prison and criminal justice policies cost our nation in lost tax dollars and lost opportunities?
- How can we better change our nation's drug policies?
- How can we better end violence in our prisons and on our city streets?
- How can we more effectively diagnose and treat mental illness, since so many of our prisoners, drug addicts, and homeless are mentally ill?
- How can we create effective re-entry programs so our communities can assimilate former offenders and encourage them to become productive citizens?
- How can we protect ourselves against the growing violence of internationally based gangs spreading through our cities? [1]

Fixes for the System

The following discussion highlights the major problems that require correction and suggested remedies.

Remedy 1: Strict Limits on Immunity of Prosecutors and Judges

Due to increasing economic pressures, justice has become a one-way revolving door wherein both judges and prosecutors seek to process cases as quickly as possible. With little incentives to seek the truth, the payoff for many prosecutors is to "win" at all costs in front of judges increasingly inclined to rule in their favor. But in any quest for efficiency rather than justice, society itself begins to suffer.

And as has been shown, civil litigation is increasingly unavailable as a deterrent against or remedy for prosecutorial misconduct — even for prosecutorial criminal conduct. With a handful of exceptions, most prosecutors do not even have written guidelines for differentiating between error and misconduct.

What can be done to ensure prosecutors act in a fair manner?

Abolish absolute immunity for prosecutors. In a 2011 *Fordham Law Review* article, Margaret Z. Johns made this call for getting rid of absolute prosecutorial immunity:

> *The doctrine of absolute prosecutorial immunity in federal civil rights actions is unsupportable. From the point of view of public policy, absolute prosecutorial immunity leads to wrongful prosecutions and convictions, ruins the lives of the wrongly accused, subjects crime victims to the painful and protracted relitigation of their experiences, impairs public safety, wastes public resources, and undermines public respect for, and confidence in, the criminal justice system.[2]*

Even conservative columnist George Will believes prosecutorial immunity should be reconsidered.[3]

Create a fair process called "qualified immunity" that would subject both prosecutors and judges to civil litigation if they are identified as having engaged in prosecutorial abuse. Immunity would be "qualified" when a prosecutor is shown to have engaged in intentional bad behavior that is not simply a mistake. It might be viewed as comparable to engaging in intentional malicious behavior, such as hiding or destroying evidence, particularly evidence the prosecutor knows would be exculpatory. Of course, the line between what is an innocent mistake and an intentional heinous act to hide or destroy evidence is subject to interpretation, which would be up to a judge.

The process of qualified immunity for prosecutors would only come into play if prosecutors have abused the process *in a criminal case,* something that would avoid the problem of litigation initiated by defendants simply unhappy with a conviction and sentence against them. The only way a victim of misconduct can maintain a civil action is to defeat any criminal charges against them and prove that "the prosecutor violated clearly established constitutional law with a culpable state of mind." Moreover, qualified immunity offers a complete defense for any prosecutorial actions except for the "most inexcusable misconduct."[4]

In short, qualified immunity would establish a basis for providing victims of intentional prosecutorial misconduct with a remedy against that misconduct. Likewise, the same kind of qualified immunity standard should be applied to judges who willfully act unfairly or with bias in a case. Since few judges are ever disciplined by judicial oversight panels, the judges engaging in misconduct should be subject to the potential for civil litigation if their behavior is shown to be egregious.

Remedy 2: Separate Courts for Urban, Suburban and Rural Areas

Most suburban voters in middle and upper income neighborhoods have little idea of ongoing abuses in the criminal justice system. Rural voters are similarly unaware since they are less likely to be affected by high crime rates. Thus, for suburban and rural constituencies alike, the criminal justice system seemingly operates in another universe: one comprising inner cities.

William J. Stuntz, an evangelical Christian and avowed conservative at Harvard Law School, claimed in *The Collapse of American Criminal Justice* that, "the American system of criminal justice has unraveled before our eyes — a phenomenon that has escaped the notice of most citizens."[5] In Stuntz's view, this lack of awareness among the general population occurred because the middle and upper classes live separate and apart from the urban poor, who are the primary targets of the criminal justice system's machinery.[5]

When those in the middle and upper classes think about how the criminal justice system works, they draw on a misleading picture presented by TV and the movies, which glamorize the police, investigators, and prosecutors. These law enforcement professionals score a win when they solve the crime and toss the criminal in jail, and virtually all criminals depicted on these shows are guilty, so the system itself is never at fault. These dramas, suspense thrillers, and action/adventure shows typically try to avoid the stereotypes that fuel racial discrimination, although such discrimination is rampant in the real day-to-day criminal justice system. The stories are unrealistic in that they do not depict the real long and drawn-out process and bureaucratic nightmare that confronts a primarily poor, inner city defendant:

> Those who have been swept within the criminal justice system know that the way the system actually

works bears little resemblance to what happens on television or in movies. Full-blown trials of guilt or innocence rarely occur; many people never even meet with an attorney; witnesses are routinely paid and coerced by the government; police regularly stop and search people for no reason whatsoever; penalties for many crimes are so severe that innocent people plead guilty, accepting plea bargains to avoid harsh mandatory sentences; and children, even as young as fourteen, are sent to adult prisons.[6]

What can be done so that prisons, and their inmates, are no longer out of sight and out of mind?

To allow for the differences in culture and customs of the urban, suburban, and rural areas, set up separate courts for urban, suburban, and rural areas in order to prosecute individuals closer to their own community of residence. (This notion was previously articulated in Chapter 13.) These separate jurisdictions might also have separate slates of prosecutors and judges so citizens vote only for the prosecutors and judges for their area. The use of separate courts in different jurisdictions might contribute to reductions in sentences and less incarceration. For example, judges in a local area might be more receptive to consider alternative sentences like halfway houses or probation rather than incarcerations.

Remedy 3: Reform the Bail Reform Act

One of the most frightening things about being arrested is a lack of ability to afford bail. Many innocent defendants simply do not have the money to pay the bail bondsman 10% of their bail, and given the drug war and rising fear about crime, the percentage of defendants granted a release on their own recognizance has shrunk to only about 15%. Although the purpose of bail is supposed to assure that the defendant will show up for court hearings (lest the bail money be forfeited), bail has become a form of punishment especially for low-income defendants, many of whom can languish in jail for months before any trial and verdict. When finally released, they may find their job, housing, property, spouse, and/or children already gone. As Albert Samaha documented in a 2012 investigative article in the *San Francisco Weekly:*

- It's the filthy secrets of the American judicial system: A majority of county jail inmates have not been convicted of any crime. They sleep and eat among the proven criminals, and are treated as such, packed in crowded barracks and transported in chains, because they did not have enough money. More than 60% of America's jail population has not been convicted, more than 70% in California...

- Those inmates are casualties of a bail system in which freedom is determined not just by a person's perceived risk to society but also by the wealth to their name....

- People who live paycheck to paycheck lose their paycheck and all that comes with it. Some lose their homes. Others lose custody of their children. Many see their family struggle to make ends meet. Banished to constitutional limbo, they see the world proceeding as their lives remain locked down and frozen. [7]

How did this unfairness come about? The Bail Reform Act of 1966 provided that defendants in non-capital crime cases have a right to be released on their own recognizance rather than bail. As necessary, a judge could impose additional conditions to make sure the person would appear in court. These had to be the least restrictive conditions possible, such as ordering a home detention, travel limitations, or a monetary bond. A pretrial incarceration was supposed to be the *last resort.*

Unfortunately, due to rising crime rates, policies changed. Law enforcement officials argued that judges should consider the "potential danger a defendant poses to society," and a number of states made public safety another consideration in setting bail. In response, Congress passed the Bail Reform Act of 1984, marking a shift from a concern with poverty and civil liberty in setting bail to assuaging the public's fear of crime and danger.[8]

So how can we do it better?

Return to the original 1966 purpose of setting bail, which was to use the least restrictive approach possible to ensure a person shows up in court. In assessing a case, judges should look at an individual's previous criminal record, if any, as well as to the strength of the case against a person. If the case hinges on a single accuser who knows the accused, that should be taken into consideration given the potential for a vindictive no-merit claim.

The judge should also consider if the person is employed, or has a partner or family in the area that might be negatively affected by the defendant being locked up. Another consideration favoring no bail or low bail might be if the person owns a home or has a long-term lease on an apartment. The judge might also issue a stay-away order to keep the defendant from having any contact with the accuser. Still another possibility is for the judge to set the bail low enough for the defendant to meet it or arrange for weekly payments.

In short, if a low-income person faces jail because he/she cannot afford bail, the judge should do everything possible to enable the defendant to remain out of jail while the case is proceeding. By doing so, the judge will avoid situations where the defendant finds their life in ruins due to time unnecessarily spent in jail awaiting trial or forced into accepting a guilty plea just to get out of jail.

Remedy 4: More Legal Assistance for Low-Income Defendants

For those without the financial means to afford an attorney to fight for them, defendants feel they have little choice but to plead guilty and accept a reduced sentence rather than risk — and likely receive — a much longer punishment. Additionally, public defenders or assigned criminal defense lawyers typically suggest a defendant take a plea, because the stark truth is that their high caseload and limited budget limits their ability to take cases to court — regardless of the case's merits. As defense attorney Michelle Alexander explains:

- Most Americans probably have no idea how common it is for people to be convicted without ever having the benefit of legal representation, or how many people plead guilty to crimes they did not commit because of fear of mandatory sentences.
- Approximately 80% of criminal defendants are indigent and thus unable to hire a lawyer. Yet our nation's public defender system is woefully inadequate. The most visible sign of the failed system is the astonishingly large caseloads public defenders routinely carry, making it impossible for them to provide meaningful representation of their clients. Sometimes defenders have well over one hundred clients at a time.[6]

As Alexander points out, both types of defense attorneys — public defenders and court-appointed private attorneys — not only are prevented from providing a good defense due to a lack of resources, but they suffer from poor working conditions and low pay, which "discourage good attorneys from participating in the system."[6]

The problem can be resolved by:

- *providing more funds to attract more public defenders and court-appointed lawyers, which in turn would allow for reduced caseloads and more time to properly handle a case.*
- *a pro bono system encouraging new lawyers to come to the aid of financially strapped clients.*

This in turn would provide an outlet for attorneys who are having difficulty finding jobs in the current economic hard times.

Remedy 5: Reduce the High Rate of Incarceration

In the United States today there are more prisoners than farmers. And while most prisoners in America are from urban communities, most prisons are now in rural areas... prisons have become a 'growth industry' in rural America.[9]

This sheer size of the prison-industrial system requires that it support a vast number of employees — about 800,000 individuals nationally. Moreover, in 2010, the annual cost to keep someone imprisoned, such as in a Federal Bureau of Prisons facility, was $28,284.16, with the annual cost of probation supervision $3,938.35.[10]

Yet despite the visions of incoming rural prosperity due to the rural prison boom, prisons are not a great boon either to the local economy, or to the inner city economy.

First, the rural prison boom pulls a substantial number of dollars from urban to rural America, because "prison inmates are counted in the populations of the towns and counties in which they are incarcerated and not in their home neighborhoods." The biggest loser? Urban communities of color, as half of all American prisoners are African-American and one-sixth Latino. These minorities' already troubled home communities therefore become even more impoverished. The communities also lose political representation and power, as prisoners can no longer vote, and yet they are counted as part of the population where they are serving time.

Rural communities lose out too, though. Surprisingly, the majority of prison jobs do not go to people already living in the community, but to others who commute there. Moreover, the mere location of a prison in a town can also discourage other kinds of industries from coming to the area.

How can we keep the sheer number of prisons, and the costs of prison maintenance and prisoner upkeep, from sapping the economies of both rural and urban communities?

We can reduce such costs through:

- *Scaling back on the War on Drugs, which has not significantly reduced the drug supply.* Scaling back will save our economy *billions.* While scaling back on inner city drug sweeps is controversial, it would reduce the number of prisoners incarcerated and the costs to incarcerate them.

- *Reducing the length of sentences given to non-violent drug offenders and defendants charged with other non-violent crimes, or offering alternative sentences based on the nature of the crime.* For example, drug offenders might be sentenced to attend drug-court programs — programs that already have proved very successful. Other options might be sentences that involve community service, participation in job training programs, or internships.

- *Sentencing convicted non-violent defendants to halfway houses, home detention, or community service programs in their home community wherever possible.*

Remedy 6: End the War on "Pot" to Reduce Violence and Bring Revenue to Cash-Starved States and Cities

As of December 6, 2012, the U.S. Federal and State Government spent *over $38 billion in the 2012 War on Drugs.*[11] Yet the war on drugs has been an utter failure, according to the Associated Press:

> *After 40 years, the United States' war on drugs has cost $1 trillion and hundreds of thousands of lives, and for what? Drug use is rampant and violence even more brutal and widespread...In the grand scheme, it has not been successful.*[12]

Although citizens associate the drug trade with crime and violence, the drugs themselves are not the cause of these activities are not caused by the drugs themselves; rather, *the crime and violence occur because drugs are illegal.* The bottom line is, "we [America'] would have a lot less violence without a war on drugs." According to economist Art Carden:

> *The war on drugs has been a dismal failure. It's high time to end prohibition. Even if you aren't willing to*

> *go whole-hog and legalize all drugs, at the very least*
> *we should legalize marijuana.*
>
> *Prohibition is a textbook example of a policy with*
> *negative unintended consequences...Vigorous*
> *enforcement means higher prices and higher*
> *revenues for drug dealers.*
>
> *The paradox is that the government's efforts to*
> *make us safer have put us in greater danger, as*
> *America's inner cities have turned into war zones*
> *and eroded the very freedoms we hold dear.[13]*

Even business writers in conservative business publications as *Forbes* have strongly advocated ending the drug wars, and at the very least, decriminalizing marijuana. This would have a huge impact on our nation: Out of the drug arrests made back in 2012, more than half (803,291) were for cannabis violations — with about 89% of those arrests for possession only.[14]

As of this writing, more than 50% of the U.S. population supports legalizing pot, and a growing number of states and cities have passed laws that make it legal to grow and distribute medical marijuana. The latest state to allow the recreational use of marijuana? Alaska.

Unfortunately, the Obama administration has waffled in its approach, initially looking the other way, and then clamping down on medicinal pot dispensaries. Most recently, it declared it would not enforce federal law in Washington and Colorado, where voters passed legislation in November 2012 to legalize marijuana for recreational use. Nationally, the debate is ongoing.

Business investors have made the case that if marijuana in all forms was legalized, it could be taxed by federal, state, and city governments, and provide significant revenue, particularly for cash-starved states and cities.

How and why should we handle the possibility of legalizing marijuana? Some possible ways include:

- *Observe closely what happens in those states that have legalized medical marijuana, and then go about legalizing it elsewhere if prudent.*
- *Decriminalize possession of small quantities of recreational marijuana to the level of a citation or speeding ticket.*

- *Legalize and tax all marijuana, and consequently invest the money that is now going toward interdiction and prison building back to government coffers.* If marijuana is legalized, it should be done in a responsible manner. Washington state's policy seems a sound one to adopt:

    1. Provide "accountable oversight by an agency of government:" A state agency will write regulations regarding the growing, producing, and selling of marijuana, to include tight limitations on advertising and the prevention of access to pot by minors. The agency will have the authority to issue licenses to growers, producers, and sellers and to enforce adherence to the rules.

    2. Include a well-funded marijuana education program based on science rather than ideology.

    3. Have a well-funded prevention program to help young people use marijuana wisely and avoid abusing it.

    4. Establish a treatment program for marijuana dependence.

    5. The law will require an evaluation of the new model's impact.

    6. State funds will be made available for research on marijuana by the state's two major research universities.[15]

Remedy 7: Establish More Drug Treatment and More Drug Courts

As noted in Remedy 6, the cost of fighting drugs over the last 40 years has been in the trillions, yet despite the U.S. devoting many resources to drug interdiction, it has not worked. More than 22 million Americans use illegal drugs as of this writing, and for most addicts, predatory crime — larceny, shoplifting, sneak thievery, burglary, embezzlement, robbery, and so forth — is a necessary way of life. **Drug addiction makes it difficult to maintain a job, and addicts often turn to crime to get the monies they need to obtain the drugs they "need" lest they suffer debilitating withdrawal symptoms.[16]**

It's time to change our approach to those who use illegal drugs, *by offering drug treatment plans rather than punishment.* From a cost-savings standpoint, drug treatment reduces expenditures. Specifically, from a criminal justice perspective, the savings to society result from less "violent and property crimes, prison expenses, court and criminal costs, emergency room visits, child abuse and neglect, lost child support, foster care and welfare costs, reduced productivity, unemployment, and victimization."[16]

Moreover, according to the National Institute of Drug Abuse (NIDA), drug treatment can "cut drug abuse in half, reduce criminal activity up to 80%, and reduce arrests up to 64%."[17] From a healthcare perspective, the spread of HIV/AIDS, hepatitis, and other infectious diseases is decreased, as such diseases are often passed on by drug addicts sharing needles.

Extensive research has shown that treatment for abusers in the criminal justice system as well as for those living outside it has proven effective. NIDA notes: "Treatment is an effective intervention for drug abusers... Longitudinal outcome studies find that those who participate in community-based drug abuse treatment programs commit fewer crimes than those who do not."[18]

Here's how we can successfully implement a new drug treatment approach:

- *Encourage sentencing changes to allow some nonviolent drug offenders out of prison early if they complete an intensive treatment program.*
- *Instead of sentencing non-violent drug offenders to prison, judges should find less restrictive penalties, such as time served coupled with treatment and probation or community service.*
- *Incorporate drug abuse treatment programs into a variety of criminal justice settings,* including treatment as a condition of probation, drug courts that combine judicial monitoring and sanctions with treatment, treatment in prison followed by community-based treatment after the individual is discharged, and treatment while the ex-convict is being supervised under parole or probation.[19]
- *Mainstream the use of drug courts for nonviolent offenders, an approach around the country that has worked by offering addicts an opportunity to participate in a treatment program along with help in finding work if they are successful in completing it.* Although only about a quarter of offenders graduate from these drug courts, those who do have greatly reduced rates of recidivism and re-arrest rates, and these programs cost our cities and states significantly less than standard prison sentences.[20-23]

Remedy 8: Overhaul the Criminal Justice System

In 2009, former Senator Jim Webb first introduced a bill urgently needed for many reasons, including these:

- With 5% of the world's population, our country now houses 25% of the world's reported prisoners.
- The number of incarcerated drug offenders has soared 1,200% since 1980.
- Four times as many mentally ill people are in prisons as in mental health hospitals.
- Approximately 1 million gang members reside in the U.S., many of them foreign-based, and Mexican cartels operate in more than 230 communities across the country.
- Post-incarceration re-entry programs are haphazard and often nonexistent, making it extremely difficult for ex-offenders to become full, contributing members of society.

Through his National Criminal Justice Commission Act (S. 306), Senator Webb sought to:

> Create a blue-ribbon commission to look at every aspect of our criminal justice system with an eye toward reshaping the criminal justice system from top to bottom …[It is] designed to prevent, deter, and reduce crime and violence, improve cost-effectiveness, and ensure the interests of justice……...It is time to bring together the best minds in America to analyze the criminal justice system in its entirety, to examine its interlocking parts, to learn what works and what does not, and make recommendations for reform."[24]

Webb's proposed bill would have created the first comprehensive national review of crime policy in 45 years. He worked tirelessly to enact the bill for three years, and lined up more than 100 key supporters in law enforcement, politics, and other fields.

Initially, his bill looked like it would do well after he received approval of the Senate Judiciary Committee on Jan. 21, 2010, and the House of Representatives passed it on July 28, 2010.

Unfortunately, the bill ran into rough waters, as it was blocked in the Senate later that year. When Webb introduced it again in February 2011, he gained support for his proposed National Criminal Justice Commission from more than 100 organizations from every political and philosophical perspective. However, the bill fell *a mere three votes short of obtaining a supermajority (sixty votes) required for passage.*[25]

Webb's bill became a victim of partisan gridlock. What should be done now? How can we do it better? There appears to be an opening.

Liberals may have gotten the "jump" on conservatives on this issue, but conservatives are finally catching up. Supreme Court Justice Anthony Kennedy, an appointee of Ronald Reagan, testified before a Financial Services and General Government Subcommittee, that "this idea of total incarceration just isn't working," and that "California, my home state, had 187,000 people in jail, at a cost of over $30,000 a prisoner, compared to the amount they gave to schoolchildren, that's about $3,500 a year."[26]

Businessman Charles Koch, oft pilloried by liberals, concludes:

> *Reversing overcriminalization and mass incarceration will improve societal well-being in many respects, most notably by decreasing poverty. Today, approximately 50 million people (about 14 percent of the population) are at or below the U.S. poverty rate. Fixing our criminal system could reduce the overall poverty rate as much as 30%, dramatically improving the quality of life throughout society — especially for the disadvantaged.*[27]

Most tellingly, the conservative Heritage Foundation identifies a number of examples of overcriminalization and concludes:

- Criminal justice reform is about more than policy debates in Congress or legal procedure; it is about how the lives and fortunes of ordinary Americans are threatened by abuse of the law. The criminal justice reform movement should focus on telling the stories of those who are affected by an overly zealous government and the excessive power of the state.
- Only by identifying the problem and highlighting why it matters will any meaningful change take place. Overcriminalization is not an easy problem to solve, but it is one that demands our attention.[28]

Webb's National Justice Commission Act is precisely what is needed to this day. Moving forward, one can only hope other legislators pick up the torch for a comprehensive overhaul of our criminal justice system, as Senator Webb has retired. Perhaps recent across-the-aisle alliances such as that between Senators Mike Lee (R), Dick Durbin (D), Ted Cruz (R), Patrick Leahy (D), and Cory Booker (D) to modernize drug sentencing guidelines,[29] or an even more comprehensive effort by Rand Paul (R) and Cory Booker (D)[30] could put such a plan forward.

It should also be noted that reducing mass incarceration cannot just be a federal effort. Since "90% of those incarcerated are in state or local facilities....mass incarceration needs to be dismantled one state at a time."[31] Thus, clearly there is a major role here for states' rights.

It may be important to accomplish significant criminal justice reform before liberals convince defendants to take truly radical action to crash the system.[32]

Bibliography

CHAPTER 10 Notes

1. Juliette Guilbert, "Why Kids Lie – An Age-by-Age Guide," Page 1 of 4, *CNN Health*, November 12, 2008. articles.cnn.com/2008-11-12/health/why.kids.lie_1_child-psychiatrist-toddlers-kids?>_s_PM:HEALTH.
2. Ibid, p. 2.
3. Marie Hartwell-Walker, "When a Child Lies," http://psychcentral.com/lib/2010/when-a-child-lies/all/1.
4. "Children and Lying, Facts for Families", *American Academy of Child & Adolescent Psychiatry*, htttp://www.aacap.org/cs/root/facts_for_families/children_and_lying.
5. Carol Roach, "Why Children Lie and How a Parent Can Deal with It," *Knoji, Consumer Knowledge*, http://child-behavior-discipline.knoji.com/why-children-lie-and-how-a-parent-can-deal-with-it
6. Dr. Phil McGraw, "When Your Child Won't Stop Lying," http://www.drphil.com/articles/print/?ArticleID=254
7. Eric-Scissorhands, "Best of, Revenge Movies," http://www.imdb.com/list/KQfm261ZTmg
8. Julie Fitness, "Betrayal, Rejection, Revenge, and Forgiveness: An Interpersonal Script Analysis," in Leary, M. (Ed.) (2001) *Interpersonal Rejection* (pp. 73-103) New York: Oxford University Press.
9. *New York Daily News*, http://www.nydailynews.com/news/national/sex-charges-dropped-alabama-assistant-principal-article-1.2044160
10. "Falsely Accused – Child Abuse," *Stop Abusive and Violent Environments*, http://www.saveservices.org/falsely-accused/child-abuse
11. Ibid.
12. Robert Suro and Bill Miller, "Perjury: A Tough Case to Make," *Washington Post*, September 24, 1998, p. A14, http://www.washingtonpost.com/wp-srv/politics/special/clinton/stories/perjury092498.htm

13. Peter Tiersma, "The Language of Perjury," http://www.languageandlaw.org/PERJURY.HTM
14. "Why Children Lie – and How to Deal with It," *Back to School Family Education,* life.familyeducation.com/parenting/lying/45311.html
15. "Lies: Why Children Lie and What to Do," *Raising Children Network,* raisingchildren.net.au/articles/lies.html
16. "Children and Lying," *Facts for Families,* No. 44, Updated November 2004, American Academy of Child & Adolescent Psychiatry, http://www.aacap.or/cs/root/facts_for_families/children_and_lying
17. James Lehman, MSW, "Why Kids Tell Lies and What to Do About It," *Empowering Parents: Child Behavior Help,* www.empoweringparents.com/article_print.php?id=10
18. "When Kids Lie," *Stanford Tutors,* http://www.freeprintablebheaviorcharts.com/lying.htm
19. Sue Watson, "Chronic Lying: How Can You Help?" *About.com Special Education* (specialed.about.com/cs/behaviordisorders/a/liar.htm?p=1
20. Carol Roach, "Why Children Lie and How a Parent Can Deal With It", https://child-behavior-discipline.knoji.com/why-children-lie-and-how-a-parent-can-deal-with-it/
21. Gini Graham Scott, *The Truth About Lying.*

CHAPTER 11 Notes

1. "Know the Laws in Your State," *Treatment Advocacy Center*, http://www.treatmentadvocacycenter.org/get-help/know-the-laws-in-your-state
2. "Emergency Hospitalization for Evaluation: Assisted Psychiatric Treatment Standards by State," *Treatment Advocacy Center*, http://treatmentadvocacycenter.org/storage/documents/Emergency_Hospitalization_for_Evaluation.pdf
3. Stephanie McCrummen, *Washington Post*, November 1, 2014, http://www.washingtonpost.com/national/a-fathers-scars-for-deeds-every-day-brings-questions/2014/11/01/2217a604-593c-11e4-8264-deed989ae9a2_story.html

CHAPTER 12 Notes

1. B. Heath and K. McCoy, "Prosecutors' conduct can tip justice scales," *USA Today*, September 23, 2010, quoted in *Studies: USA Today Investigation Reveals Prosecutorial Misconduct in Federal Cases*. http://deathpenaltyinfo.org/studies-usa-today-investigation-reveals-prosecutorial-misconduct-federal-cases

2. Kathleen Ridolfi and Maurice Possley "Preventable Error: A Report on Prosecutorial Misconduct in California 1997-2009", http://digitalcommons.law.scu.edu/ncippubs/2/

3. Ken Armstrong and Maurice Possley, "Part I: The verdict: Dishonor", *Chicago Tribune*, January 11, 1999, http://www.chicagotribune.com/news/watchdog/chi-020103trial1,0,479347.story

4. Barry Scheck, "Errant Prosecutors Seldom Held to Account", *The Innocence Project*, May 7, 2012, http://www.innocenceproject.org/news-events-exonerations/errant-prosecutors-seldom-held-to-account

5. Chuck Neubauer, "Senator rips misconduct in Stevens case", *Washington Times*, March 28, 2012, http://www.washingtontimes.com/news/2012/mar/28/senator-prosecutorial-misconduct-stevens-case-cann/?page=all

6. Stuart Taylor and K.C. Johnson, *Until Proven Innocent: Political Correctness and the Shameful Injustices of the Duke Lacrosse Rape Case*, St. Martin's Griffin, 2008.

7. "Duke Lacrosse Sexual Assault Case," *New York Times*, June 22, 2012, topics.nytimes.com/topics/reference/timestopics/organizations/d/duke_university/.../index.html

8. "Falsely-accused Duke Lacrosse Players Seek Millions, Reforms," *EPSN.com*, Sept. 7, 2007, espn.go.com/espn/print?id=3008460&type=story

9. "Fabricated Evidence in Criminal Cases," *The Stopped Clock*, September 7, 2011, http://the stoppedclock.blogspot.com/2011/09/fabricated-evidence-in-criminal-cases.html

10. Jeff Stanglin, "Prosecutorial Misconduct is a Crime: Attorneys Who Are Guilty Should Be Punished, June 30, 2008,

http://suite101.com/article/prosecutorial-misconduct-is-a-crime-a58867, accessed June 17, 2012.

11. Heather Schoenfeld, "Violated Trust: Conceptualizing Prosecutorial Misconduct," *Journal of Contemporary Criminal Justice*, August 2004, Vol. 21. No. 3. 250-271, Abstract.

12. Mark Donald: Texas Lawyer, A Justice-at-All-Costs Attitude--Impact Player of the Year Craig Watkins, *Truth in Justice*, December 24, 2007; www.truthinjustice.org/craig-watkins.htm

CHAPTER 13 Notes

1. David E. Danda, "Complaints Against Judges," *FindLaw for Legal Professionals*, Jan 1, 2001, library.findlaw.com/2001/Jan/1/129441html
2. http://www.judgejudy.com/
3. Michael Paul Thomas, "Judicial Misconduct: Judges Behaving Badly, *Daily Journal*, www.dailyjournal.com/cle.cfm?show=CLEDisplayArticles&qVersionID=85&eid=821923&evid=1
4. Hans Sherrer in "The Complicity of Judges in the Generation of Wrongful Convictions", *Northern Kentucky Law Review*, Vol. 30:4j.
5. Richard Klein, "Judicial Misbehavior in Criminal Cases: It's Not Just the Counsel Who May Be Ineffective and Unprofessional," *Ohio State Journal of Criminal Law, Vol 4: 195*, 2006.
6. Cynthia Gray, "The Line Between Legal Error and Judicial Misbehavior: Balancing Judicial Independence and Accountability," *Hofstra Final,* November 24, 2004.
7. Gary Hunter and Alex Friedmann, *Prison Legal News*, June 26, 2012, https://www.prisonlegalnews.org/(S(xsnmk4qmegola055ovintkns))/displayArticle.aspx?articleid=21570
8. William J. Stuntz, *The Collapse of American Criminal Justice*, 2011, The Belknap Press of Harvard Univ. Press, p. 7.

CHAPTER 14 Notes

1. Jaime N. Morris: "The Anonymous Accused: Protecting Defendants' Rights in High-Profile Criminal Cases," (44 B.C.L. Rv 901 (2003)), http:/lawdigitalcommons.bc.edu/bclr/vol44/iss3/6.
2. Douglas O. Linder, *The Dr. Sam Sheppard Trial*, 2006 http://law2.umkc.edu/faculty/projects/ftrials/sheppard/sheppardacc ount.html
3. "Chapter Seven: Press and Fair Trial," www.radford.edu/wkovarik/class/law/1.7/fairtrial.htm
4. "The Sam Sheppard Murder Case, *About.com Guide*, About.com Crime/Punishment, crime.about.com/od/history/p/sheppard_sam.htm.
5. Judicial Studies Board, "Reporting Restrictions in the Crown Court," http://www.societyofeditors.co.uk/userfiles/file/Reporting Restrictions Crown Court.pdf
6. http://www.washingtonpost.com/blogs/erik-wemple/wp/2015/01/22/e-mails-reflect-massive-impact-of-discredited-rolling-stone-story-on-u-va/
7. http://content.time.com/time/specials/2007/la_riot/article/0,28804,1 614117_1614084_1614831,00.html
8. http://law2.umkc.edu/faculty/projects/ftrials/Simpson/simpson.htm
9. http://www.nytimes.com/2013/07/14/us/george-zimmerman-verdict-trayvon-martin.html?_r=0
10. http://www.nytimes.com/interactive/2014/08/13/us/ferguson-missouri-town-under-siege-after-police-shooting.html?_r=0
11. http://www.nydailynews.com/new-york/nypd-eric-garner-chokehold-death-not-indicted-article-1.2031841
12. Race to Judgment: Stereotyping Media and Criminal Defendants (*Law and Contemporary Problems, Vol. 71:93, 2008),* Robert M. Entman and Kimberly Gross pp. 95-103, 128
13. Kevin Sack, "Richard Jewell, 44, Hero of Atlanta Attack, Dies," *The New York Times, August 30, 2007.* http://www.nytimes.com/2007/08/30/us/30jewell.html
14. David Freed, "The Wrong Man," *The Atlantic*, May 2010, p. 2. www.theatlantic.com/magazine/print/2010/05/the-wrong-man/8019

15. http://www.tv.com/shows/charlie-rose/watch/marion-cotillard-andrew-solomon-a-discussion-about-prison-reform-2615132/
16. http://www.pbs.org/independentlens/house-i-live-in/
17. http://www.texasmonthly.com/topics/michael-morton
18. Michael Morton, "Getting Life: An Innocent Man's 25-Year Journey from Prison to Peace," Simon & Schuster, 2014.
19. http://ffilms.org/west-of-memphis-2012/
20. http://www.pbs.org/kenburns/centralparkfive/

CHAPTER 15 Notes

1. David Packman, "Putting Police Misconduct Statistics in Perspective," *The Cato Institute's Project*, October 28, 2009, http://www.policemisconduct.net/putting-police-misconduct-statistics-in-perspective

2. S.E. Smith, "What was the Rampart scandal?" *WiseGeek*, http://www.wisegeek.com/what-was-the-rampart-scandal.htm

3. Renford Reese, *The Multiple Causes of the LAPD Rampart Scandal*, California State Polytechnic Institute, Pomona, California, Fall, 2003, http://www.csupomona.edu/~jis/2003/Reese.pdf

4. CNN Justice, "Ex-L.A. cop sentenced to 5 years," August 7, 2002, http://articles.cnn.com/2002-08-07/justice/rampart.sentencing_1_corruption-scandal-officer-nino-durden-police-officer?_s=PM:LAW

5. 392 U.S. 1, https://supreme.justia.com/us/392/1/case.html (1968)

6. Laura Scarry, "Stop & Identify: Can an officer arrest a suspect for failing to provide ID?", *Law Officer Magazine*, October 27, 2005; http://www.policeone.com/columnists/Iom/articles/120321-Stop-Identify-Can-an-officer-arrest-a-suspect-for-failing-to-produce-ID

7. Clay White, "Failure to Identify to a Police Officer: Laws and Penalties", *Criminal Defense Lawyer.com*; http://www.criminaldefenselawyer.com/crime-penalties/federal/Failure-identify-police-officer.htm

8. http://apps.washingtonpost.com/g/documents/national/department-of-justice-report-on-the-ferguson-mo-police-department/1435/

9. Rich Stim, "Overview of Search and Seizure Laws," *CriminalDefenseLawyer.com*, http://www.criminaldefenselawyer.com/resources/criminal-defense-case/overview-search-and-seizure-laws.htm

10. Independent Lens 4/8/13

11. http://www.theguardian.com/us-news/video/2014/dec/04/i-cant-breathe-eric-garner-chokehold-death-video
12. http://www.columbia.edu/itc/journalism/cases/katrina/Human_Rights_Watch/uspohtml/uspo34.htm
13. Demian Bulwa, "BART pays $1.5 million to aid Grant's daughter, SF Gate, *San Francisco Chronicle*, January 28, 2010, http://www.sfgate.com/bayarea/article/BART-pays-1-5-million-to-aid-Grant-s-daughter-3201450.php
14. Radley Balko, "The War on Cameras," *Reason.com*, January 2011, http://reason.com/archives/2010/12/07/the-war-on-cameras/4

CHAPTER 16 Notes

1. http://www.people.com/people/archive/article/0,,20580704,00.html
2. Creasie Finney Hairston "*Prisoners and Families: Parenting Issues During Incarceration*", Jane Addams College of Social Work, University of Illinois at Chicago, December 2001, http://aspe.hhs.gov/hsp/prison2home02/hairston.htm
3. Philip Genty "Incarcerated Parents and the Adoption and Safe Families Act ("ASFA"): A Challenge for Correctional Service Providers" ICCA Journal on Community Corrections, November 2001, 42-47.
4. Jeremy Travis and Michelle Waul, "*Prisoners Once Removed: The Impact of Incarceration on Children, Families, and Communities*", Urban Institute, 2004.
5. Kate Adamson, Flynn Carey, Jean Nash, Ryan Flynn, Josh Baker, Rimal Popat, *Collateral Consequences of Criminal Conviction in Arizona*, Preliminary Discussion Draft, AZCCStudy8.9.2005.pdf
6. Stop Abusive and Violent Environments study, "*How False Allegations Harm Families and Children*", p. 6.
7. Second Chance Coalition Principle, "*Families with Incarcerated Parents Fact Sheet*"
8. Pew Social and Demographic Trends, Pew Research Center, "College Enrollment Hits an All Time High, Fueled by Community College Surge", http://www.pewsocialtrends.org/2009/10/29/college-enrollment-hits-all-time-high-fueled-by-community-college-surge
9. Bureau of Labor Statistics, Table 1A. Employment status of the civilian population by sex and age, http://www.bls.gov/news.release.empsit.t01.htm
10. http://www.projectreturninc.org/about/index.html

CHAPTER 17 Notes

1. Steven Nolan, "The Prison Industrial Complex", *The Intelhub.com*; http://theintelhub.com/2012/05/17prison-industrial-complex
2. Robert A. Ferguson, *Inferno: An Anatomy of American Punishment*, Harvard University Press, 2014.
3. Michelle Alexander, *The New Jim Crow: Mass Incarceration in the Age of Colorblindness*, The New Press, 2012.
4. Charlie Rose; http://www.tv.com/shows/charlie-rose/watch/marion-cotillard-andrew-solomon-a-discussion-about-prison-reform-2615132/
5. David Wolman, "The New Economics of Crime and Punishment", *Wired*, November 2011, http://www.wired.com/2012/11/st_essay_convictonomics/
6. Ed Morrisey, "Sessions: Food Stamps Programs Expanding in Costs, Size," *Hot Air*; http://hotair.com/archives/2012/06/27/sessions-food-stamp-programs-exploding-in-costs-size/
7. James Webb, "What's Wrong with Our Prisons?" *Parade*, March 29, 2009, p. 5
8. "1 in 3 Black Men Go To Prison? The 10 Most Disturbing Facts About Racial Inequality in the U.S. Criminal Justice System". *AlterNet*, March 17, 2012.
9. "Families with Incarcerated Parents Fact Sheet."
10. "The Caging of America: Why Do We Lock So Many People Up," (*The New Yorker,* January 30, 2012; http://www.newyorker.com/arts/critics/atlarge/2012/01/30/120130crat_atlarge_gopnik
11. Office of Policy Planning and Research, United States Department of Labor, "The Negro Family: The Case for National Action", March 1965; http://www.intellectualtakeout.org/content/quotes-welfare-state-family
12. Erik Eckholm, "With Higher Numbers of Prisoners Comes a Tide of Troubled Children," *New York Times* (July 5, 2009).
13. Roy Ockert, "Study offers suggestions to keep prison inmates from returning," *The Pine Bluff Commercial*, December 19, 2014, http://pbcommercial.com/columns-blogs/roy-ockert/study-offers-suggestions-keep-prison-inmates-returning

14. Federal Court Programs Threatened by Budget Cuts, Official Warns Congress, The BLT, Blog of Legal Times: Law and Lobbying in the Nation's Capital, March 28, 2012, http://legaltimes.typepad.com/blt/2012/03/federal-courts-programs-threatened-by-budget-cuts-official-warns-congress.html

15. Andrew Cohen, "At State Courts, Budgets Are Tight and Lives are In Limbo", The Atlantic, September 23, 2011, http://www.theatlantic.com/national/archive/2011/09/at-state-courts-budgets-are-tight-and-lives-are-in-limbo/245558/#

CHAPTER 18 Notes

1. James Webb, "It's time to change the law", *Parade*, http://parade.com/104193/senatorjimwebb/its-time-to-change-the-law/ and "Why me must fix our prisons", *Parade*, http://parade.com/104227/senatorjimwebb/why-we-must-fix-our-prisons/
2. Margaret Z. Johns, "Unsupportable and Unjustified: A Critique of Absolute Prosecutorial Immunity", *Fordham Law Review* 80 (2011); http://ir.lawnet.fordham.edu/cgi/viewcontent.cgi?article=4662&context=flr
3. George Will, "Overcriminalization plagues U.S. Society"; *Tyler Morning Telegraph*, April 9, 2015; http://www.tylerpaper.com/TP-Editorials/217392/overcriminalization-plagues-us-society
4. Margaret Z. Johns, "Reconsidering Absolute Prosecutorial Immunity", *Brigham Young University Law Review* (3/1/2005) http://digitalcommons.law.byu.edu/cgi/viewcontent.cgi?article=2225&context=lawreview
5. Eric Pilch, "Criminal Injustice," *Counterpoint: A Magazine of Politics and Culture*, April 19, 2012, http://www.counterpointmagazine.org/2012/04/19/criminal-injustice
6. Michelle Alexander, *The New Jim Crow: Mass Incarceration in the Age of Colorblindness,* The New Press, 2012.
7. Albert Samaha, "Barred from Freedom: How Pretrial Detention Ruins Lives", *San Francisco Weekly*, November 21, 2012; http://www.sfweekly.com/sanfrancisco/barred-from-freedom-how-pretrial-detention-ruins-lives/Content?oid=2187112
8. *John Goldkamp* "Danger and Detention: A Second Generation of Bail Reform", *Journal of Criminal Law and Criminology*, 76(1), 1985, pp. *1-74.*
9. Tracy Huling, "Building a Prison Economy in Rural America," from *Invisible Punishment,* Marc Mauer and Meda Chesney-Lind, Editors. The New Press. 2002, http://www.prisonpolicy.org/scans/building.html

10. "Newly Available: Costs of Incarceration and Supervision in FY 2010" *The Third Branch News, United States Courts*, June 23, 2011, http://tinyurl.com/apyw4qh

11. "The Drug War Clock, December 6, 2012, citing the Office of National Drug Control Policy, and Jeffrey A. Miron & Kathrine Waldock, "The Budgetary Impact of Drug Prohibition," 2010.

12. "AP IMPACT: After 40 years, $1 trillion, US War on Drugs has failed to meet any of its goals." *Fox News.com*, May 13, 2010, http://tinyurl.com/apngetu

13. Art Carden, "Let's Be Blunt: It's Time to End the Drug War." http://tinyurl.com/a98cpyz

14. "The Drug War Clock citing Uniform Crime Reports, Federal Bureau of Investigation," http://www.drugsense.org/cms/wodclock

15. "The End of the War on Marijuana", *CNN*, November 9, 2012, http://www.cnn.com/2012/11/08/opinion/roffman-pot-legalization/index.html

16. "Drug Addiction, Crime or Disease?" *Interim and Final Reports of the Joint Committee of the American Bar Association and the American Medical Association on Narcotic Drugs.* http://www.druglibrary.org/schaffer/library/studies/dacd/appendixa_9.htm

17. "NIDA Announces Recommendations to Treat Drug Abusers, Save Money and Reduce Crime", *NIH News*, July 24, 2006; http://www.nih.gov/news/pr/jul2006/nida-24.htm

18. "Principles of Drug Abuse Treatment for Criminal Justice Populations – A Research-Based Guide," *National Institute of Drug Abuse, National Institutes of Health*, http://tinyurl.com/bc5aco9

19. "DrugFacts: Treatment for Drug Abusers in the Criminal Justice System, Revised July 2006, http://tinyurl.com/by8kb7p

20. "Drug Court Helps Addicts Kick Habit – and Charges," *San Francisco Chronicle*, November 12, 2012, pp. A1, A9, http://www.sfgate.com/crime/article/Drug-court-Addicts-kick-habit-charges-4028550.php

21. San Francisco Collaborative Courts, *Research Review*, May 2009.

22. State of New Jersey, Office of the Public Defender, http://www.state.nj.us/defender/drugcrt.shtml

23. John Rodor, Wendy Townsend, and Avinash Sing Bhati: *Recidivism Rates for Drug Court Graduates: Nationally Based*

Estimates, Final Report, July, 2003;
https://www.ncjrs.gov/pdffiles1/201229.pdf

24. http://www.humanejustice.org/background_criminal_justice.htm

25. http://sentencing.typepad.com/sentencing_law_and_policy/2011/10
/senate-republicans-block-jim-webbs-bill-for-creating-national-criminal-justice-commission.html

26. Jess Bravin, "Two Supreme Court Justices Say Criminal-Justice Syustem Isn't Working," *The Wall Street Journal*, March 24, 2015.

27. Charles G. Koch and Mark V. Holden, "The Overcriminalization of America. How to reduce poverty and improve race relations by rethinking our justice system." *Politico Magazine*, January 7, 2015;
http://www.politico.com/magazine/story/2015/01/overcriminalizati on-of-america-113991.html#.VXXcU03bKUk

28. Jordan Richardson, "Shining a Light on Overcriminalization", *The Heritage Foundation*, June 1, 2015;
http://www.heritage.org/research/reports/2015/06/shining-a-light-on-overcriminalization

29. http://www.lee.senate.gov/public/index.cfm/2015/2/lee-durbin-introduce-smarter-sentencing-act-of-2015

30. http://www.paul.senate.gov/?p=press_release&id=1192

31. Michelle Alexander, "Go to Trial: Crash the Justice System," *The New York Times, Sunday Review*, The Opinion Pages, March 10, 2012; http://tinyurl.com/avo9rjb

32. Marc Mauer and David Cole, "How to Lock Up Fewer People," *New York Times*, May 24, 2015.